"The mind is nothing like what you've been taught to believe. There are many different access routes into it, and understanding its overall simplifications and policies can make you operate better and more effectively manage yourself and your own thought processes, as well as manage other people."

- from MindReal

This is a book that shows, in simple detail, one of the most startling findings of modern science: **We don't experience the world as it is, but as virtual reality.** And while much of the latest scientific work demonstrates this, as do many of the classical psychological illusions, it is an important meeting point for students of the mind, brain, philosophy and religion because, as we can now see in light of this book, all these disciplines begin at the same place.

This is not an abstruse treatise, but part graphic novel and part direct address. It allows the reader a breakthrough understanding of the mind which is not available anywhere else. It is, in part, a summa of Dr. Ornstein's research and writing of the past 35 years (with pieces and references to many of his works) as well as a seminal introduction to new readers.

MINDREAL

How the mind creates
its own
virtual reality

ROBERT ORNSTEIN, PHD, was an award-winning psychologist, pioneering brain researcher, and author or co-author of over 20 books on the nature of the human mind and brain and their relationship to thought, health and individual and social consciousness. His books have sold over six million copies, been used in 20,000 university classes worldwide, and been translated into dozens of languages.

His groundbreaking books *The Psychology of Consciousness* and *The Evolution of Consciousness* introduced the two modes of consciousness of the left and right brain hemispheres, and a critical understanding how the brain evolved. Ornstein considered these, along with *God 4.0: On the Nature of Higher Consciousness and the Experience called "God"* (forthcoming 2021), his most important writings. The three books together provide a fundamental reconsideration of ancient religious and spiritual traditions in the light of advances in brain science and psychology, exploring the potential and relevance of this knowledge to contemporary needs and to our shared future.

Dr. Ornstein taught at the University of California Medical Center and Stanford University, and lectured at more than 200 colleges and universities in the U.S. and overseas. He was the president and founder of the Institute for the Study of Human Knowledge (ISHK), an educational nonprofit dedicated to bringing important discoveries concerning human nature to the general public. Among his many honors and awards are the UNESCO award for Best Contribution to Psychology and the American Psychological Foundation Media Award "for increasing the public understanding of psychology."

Ornstein's ground-breaking research and writing on the specialization of the brain's left and right hemispheres, on the multiple nature of our mind and its untapped potential for solving contemporary problems, has advanced our understanding of who we are, how we got here and how we might evolve to the benefit of ourselves and our planet.

ALSO BY TED DEWAN

Inside the Whale and Other Animals
(with Steve Parker)

Inside Dinosaurs and Other Prehistoric Creatures
(with Steve Parker)

3 Billy Goats Gruff

Top Secret

The Sorcerer's Apprentice

The Weatherbirds

Crispin the Pig Who Had It All

Baby Gets the Zapper

wormworks.com

TED DEWAN received his degree in engineering from Brown University in 1983 and taught physics at Milton Academy in Boston. Now living in London, his illustrations have appeared in *The Times*, *The Guardian*, and *The Independent*. He is best known as a children's author/illustrator and has received the Mother Goose Award as well as being shortlisted for The Kurt Maschler and The Kate Greenaway Awards. He has also created the website **wormworks.com**.

MIND REAL

• • •

How the mind creates its own virtual reality

by Robert Ornstein
illustrations by Ted Dewan

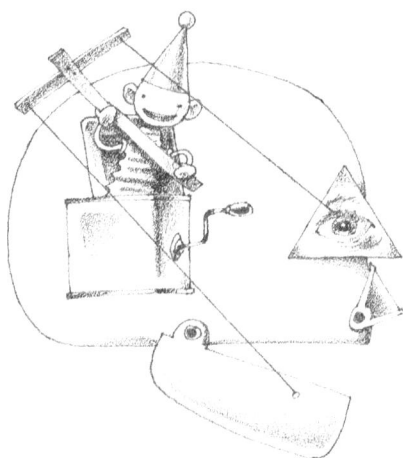

Interspersed with segments of

THE MIND REAL TOUR

by Ted Dewan

MALOR BOOKS
Los Altos CA

Malor Books is an imprint of
The Institute for the Study of Human Knowledge

For Sally
for all the times, support and help.

R. O.

●

For Helen
Protector of Sanity

T. D.

...human kind
cannot bear very much reality.

-- T. S. Eliot, "Burnt Norton"

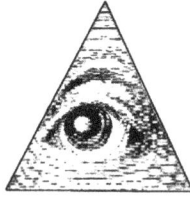

CONTENTS

THE
MindReal
TOUR

·

ACKNOWLEDGEMENTS

Of course there are the collaborators on books that lead to *MindReal*: David Sobel, Paul Ehrlich, Charles Swencionis. And all of us are grateful to the immense research work that has revolutionized the study of the mind. On this book, I'm supported, daily, by Shane De Haven and Sally Mallam in getting the book into physical shape, and it benefited from a close read and many corrections by Dan Sperling, and by the help of Aldo Lira. Ted Dewan designed it and did his own inimitable bit, in a great "Mindreal."

Robert Ornstein, 2008

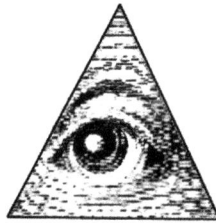

PREFACE

Let's make it clear: there is a world out there, and there is a world in here. It's not like "east is east and west is west, and never the twain shall meet," for if they never met, then we wouldn't be alive. Think of it as two overlapping circles; a thin ellipse at the intersection is where the mind and world join. There's more to the world than we experience, obviously -- the galaxies, the subatomic world. We "catch," for instance, only one-trillionth of the waves that dazzle our eye.

I see this book as a beginning. It may be a real beginning for someone who hasn't thought about the mind, or psychology, or philosophy. It may be a second, third or fourth beginning for another who has had some interest.

At the core of these realms, and of religion and consciousness as well, is this: our "reality" isn't the reality of the world, but a tiny portion of it. This means, in one view, that we're subject to illusions and misjudgments; in another, that true knowledge is very, very difficult; and in a third, that the "world" is an "illusion."

However, realizing that the reality we experience is "Mind-Real" is the first step to a deeper understanding of ourselves, and of our possibilities.

Fear not: this won't be a philosophical conundrum or some kind of epic esoteric treatise. My aim is to make the feeling of *MindReal* clear in terms of both everyday and, like many of our media now, even in graphic novel (well, graphic nonfiction) form.

Robert Ornstein, 2008

0

THE WORLD WE TOUCH, SEE AND HEAR IS NOT THE "REAL" WORLD

I was sitting late at night overlooking the lake with my wife and two friends -- psychiatrists, as it turns out. It was a quiet scene. We were eating snacks after a show, outside in a café with a good view of a long stretch of cool water and Italian homes overlooking it.

Then, all of a sudden, we were surrounded by the sounds of three tenors in high aria, and the "lake" erupted into a water show, with plumes of water shooting up into the night, 60 feet high. Illuminated, of course.

A jolt.

We were not by Lake Como. The restaurant was not an Italian trattoria, but a New York steakhouse. And at the other side of the lake in the desert was…not an Italian villa, not even a New York street, but…

The Eiffel Tower!

How completely unreal. New York, Italy, Paris -- all in the Las Vegas desert.

It's a cause for amazement, yet…

Of course, this particular jumble of structures only seems un-real; but it is, of course, real. It's there. Las Vegas is one sort of "reality," but I mention it here because sitting there, I could see that this amalgam, or "shell game," of different experiences is exactly what happens inside us each moment. If Las Vegas is unreal in some sense, is our "reality" unreal, too? I want to as-sert here that it is exactly so, made up each moment of a shell game of different images and experiences, put together not to experience the world, but, like another kind of shell, to protect us while in the world.

And it's true of the built world as well. What was "real" about the New York skyscrapers before they were built on $14 worth of land; didn't they seem "unreal"? The Eiffel Tower, too, was ridiculed as being an idiotic, pointless structure. We now see it as the symbol of Paris, but if you look at it, what is it but a bunch of ironwork? (It is really a demo, an ad for an iron fabrication company.) The French first called it an "iron asparagus."

And my Las Vegas experience happened at the same time that a biography of Ronald Reagan had been published which featured imaginary characters to create a fuller truth, the author said.

That -- a virtual scene like the one in Las Vegas or the fleshing out of a narrative with imaginary characters to make it fit -- is what we do each moment of each day.

Our "reality,"
the one we live inside,
is virtual.
We call it
"MindReal."

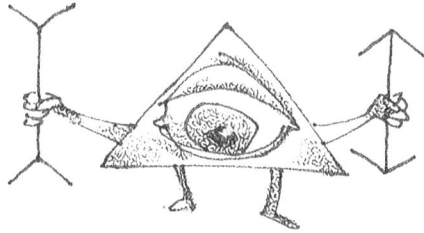

THE
MindReal
TOUR

·

Am 'I Am,' or
Am I MindReal?

YOU THINK, THEREFORE I AM...

YOU THINK, THEREFORE I AM... OR AM I?

(sigh) You waste so much *time* navel-gazing, don't you...

Don't *you* think that's a pretty important question? And who *are* you, anyhow?

Hmmf--you're much too *self-obsessed* to pay much attention to *me* anymore, but you used to call me "*The Supreme Being*," To be honest, I'm not feeling so *supreme* these days.

Hey, what's the matter? You sound pretty *fed up*. Did I do something wrong?

Hmmm, I suppose so, but it's my own damn fault. You see...well, maybe it's time I let you in on one of the big *secrets* I've been keeping from you and your kind for *eons*. Maybe it will help.

MIND LTD

That would be *swell* if you could give me a clue. After all, if I've been waiting eons, there's no time like the *present* for sorting me out.

Hmmmf--how *true*, my friend, how *true*. You see, you may *think* consciousness is everything, and you're in control, but you'll soon see there's *far more* going on in your subconscious than you ever *imagined*.

MIND LTD.

Back when I was experimenting with *micro-organisms*, it all seemed like life was going to be simple--just wind the things up and watch 'em go. All they needed from *Reality* was the right conditions and a few *chemicals* now and then. They had *little idea* what was going on *outside* their tiny little worlds.

But when microorganisms started *getting together* to form larger organisms, they made *new* problems for themselves. In order to survive, they needed to process *more* information from *Reality* than they did back in the single-cell days.

HOW
SO? ———

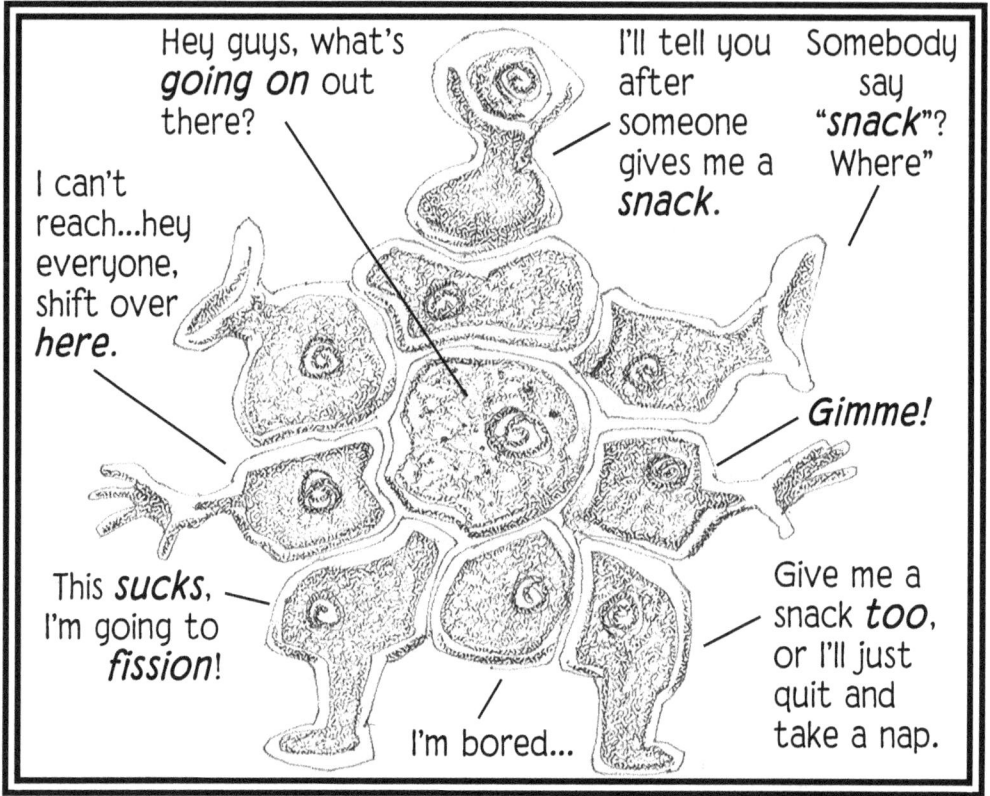

See, like any *organization*, the *bigger* it gets, the *more management* it needs. And it also needs *more* admin, specialization and communication. The ability and reach of the agglomeration get *bigger* and so does the *hunger for information*. They got together to form some terrific instruments for receiving information from the outside world.

Of course, then they had to develop wetware *sophisticated* enough to distinguish what was important for *survival*--and *Mind LTD* was formed.

Mind LTD is like *one big company.* Like *any* big company, the workers work in far-from-harmonious conditions. There are *crazy* and *outdated policies*, plenty of vying for space, lies and deceit, massive *ignorance*, and *plenty* of *screwing up.*

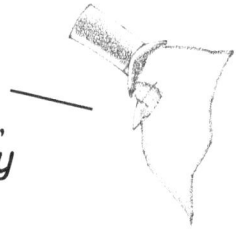

BILLIONS OF BITS OF INFORMATION...

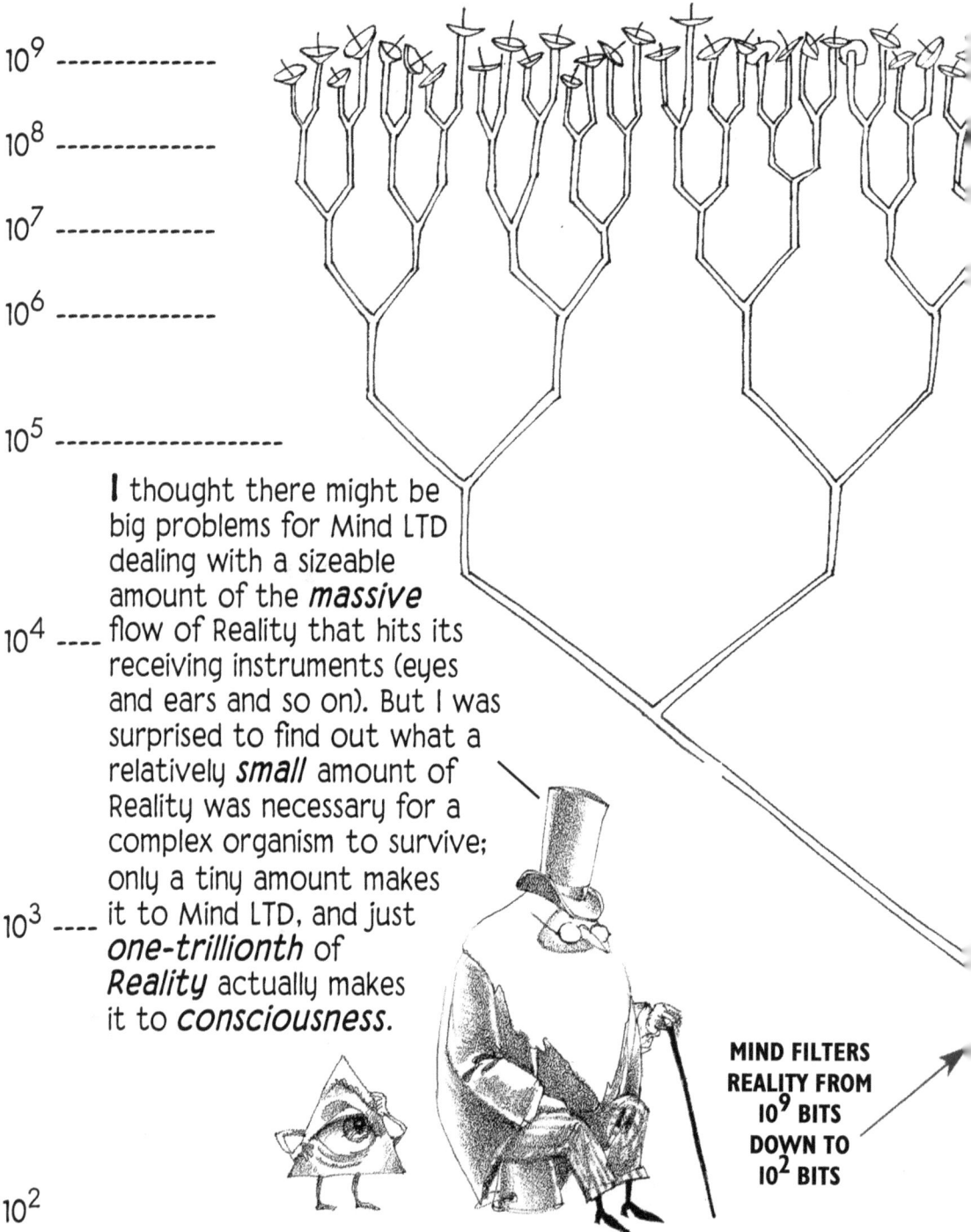

10^9 -------------

10^8 -------------

10^7 -------------

10^6 -------------

10^5 ------------------

10^4 ---- I thought there might be big problems for Mind LTD dealing with a sizeable amount of the *massive* flow of Reality that hits its receiving instruments (eyes and ears and so on). But I was surprised to find out what a relatively *small* amount of Reality was necessary for a complex organism to survive; only a tiny amount makes

10^3 ---- it to Mind LTD, and just *one-trillionth* of *Reality* actually makes it to *consciousness*.

MIND FILTERS REALITY FROM 10^9 BITS DOWN TO 10^2 BITS

10^2

...COMING IN FROM REALITY EVERY SECOND

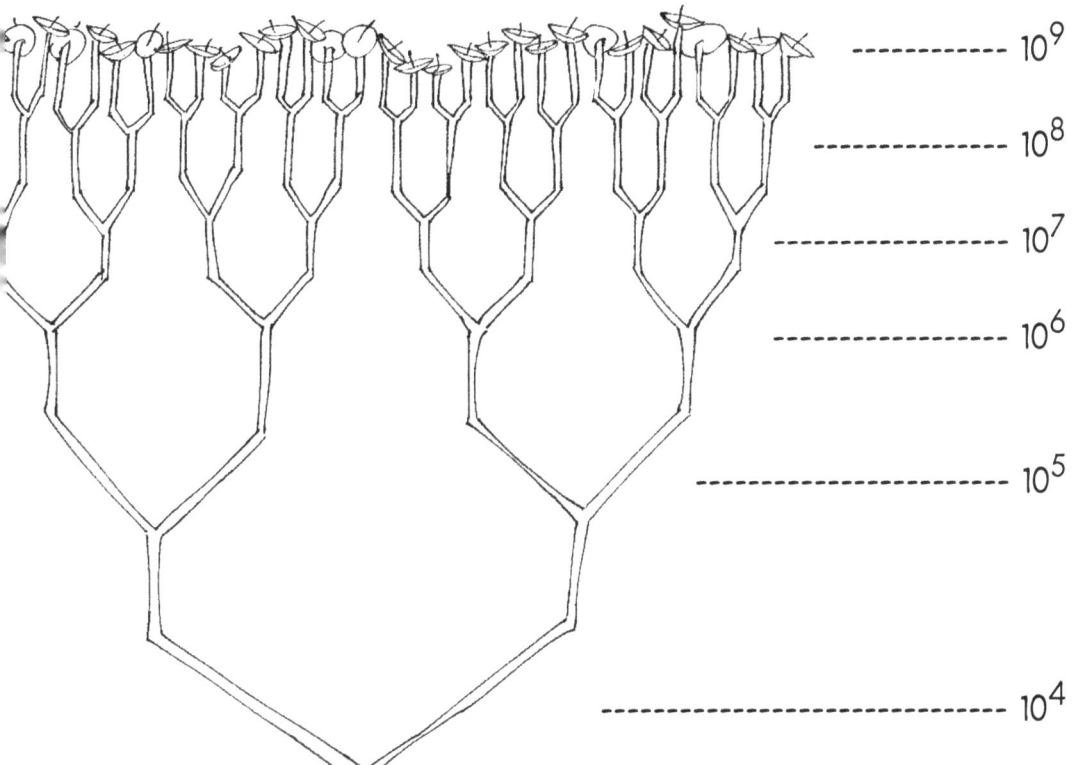

----------- 10^9

-------------- 10^8

----------------- 10^7

-------------------- 10^6

---------------------- 10^5

------------------------------ 10^4

With such a *tiny fraction* of Reality to cope with, you managed fine. Mind LTD and its receiving instruments could filter the great thicket of *Reality* into progressively thinner strands, doing all the *dirty work* for consciousness.

10^3

10^2

The reduced and filtered
strands of Reality then
become *woven together*
by a multitude of little
automatic workers to form
a tapestry of *illusion*.
So instead of actually
experiencing the full force
of Reality, which would
overwhelm even the most
sophisticated computer
imaginable...

...*Mind LTD* makes up its own notion of what's real--*MINDREAL.*

But...but that's *ridiculous.* You mean to say that *I make up* Reality?

REALITY

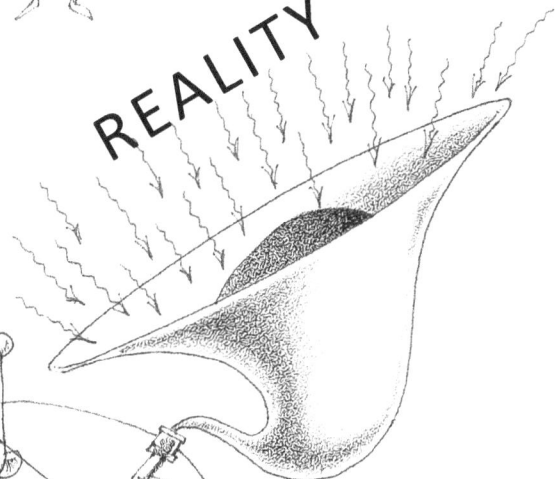

Believe it or not, I'm *Reality*!

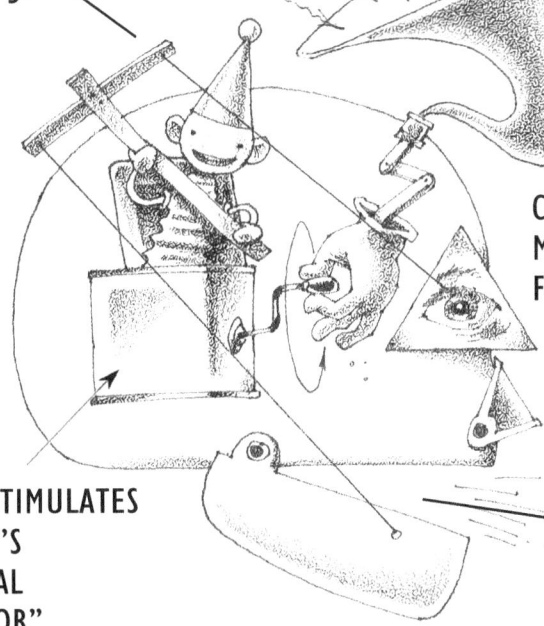

CONSCIOUSNESS MISTAKES MINDREAL FOR REALITY

FILTERED REALITY STIMULATES MIND LTD'S "MINDREAL GENERATOR"

Silly! Of *course* you are!

No, you don't *make up* Reality. *Reality* is *really* out there. But what you *believe* to be *real* is actually only *MindReal*. You are completely *immersed* in a tiny chamber of total *self-delusion*.

MINDREAL

Now you're **blowin' _my_** _mind_, pops...

Er, _forgive me_, that's probably a bit _too much information_ all at once...

ALL YOU ARE
IS WHAT YOU ARE
DURING THE MOMENT
YOU ARE IT

-- *Graffiti, New York Subway, 1993*

I

•

How the Mind Transforms the World: The Life of the Mind

ABOUT THE EYE BLINK
THE NOSE
THE PHANTOM FINGER
THE "SHELL"
"BROWN MONDAYS"
AND THE WORLD'S IMPERCEPTIBLE THICKET

What the mind does seems so obvious that we never need to think about it. Our experience of the world seems, as we experience it from inside our head, seamless: the mind gets the basic information about sounds, location of objects, the nature of people and the like from the world outside and prepares us to act. It feels seamless at second glance and over a lifetime, as well.

And as far as "we" are concerned, throughout almost all of our everyday life, it works just fine and dandy. One of our friends calls on the telephone; we immediately remember who he is and what our conversations have been. We don't confuse conversations we've had with Peter with those we've had with Juliet. We see a dog running towards us and avoid it; smell dinner cooking on the stove and, sure enough, the meatloaf is there, ready to be eaten when we get into the house. We see the rain outside when dressing, and, sure enough, when we go out, it hits us on the face and wets our boots. We see and sense what is going on and act accordingly. Doesn't really seem like much of a conundrum in our daily experiences. No big deal, right?

It's difficult to see the problem from *inside* our own mind. We can't picture "the mind," as can we the heart, the brain or the liver. The mind isn't a corporeal structure and it isn't identical to the brain or any other physical entity. And its invisible work is profound: it connects the sounds, sights and signs of the external world into entities that we see, feel and touch. It does this continually, and its operations are in our consciousness rarely and momentarily. What we call "Mental Operating System" (MOS) processes are at the root of unnoticed daily triumphs in navigating a complex world. Conversely, this is why things that are always visible to us can't be seen (like the nose), and why the simplifying MOS routines are at the roots of many errors we make. We most often have to make decisions based on incomplete information.

The mind's primary job is not intellectual, so the "life of the mind" is not the serious life that this phrase usually indicates. Rather, it is the hidden work of a magician: to present the person with a set of illusions that work. The tricky thing is this: we experience these reactions as our consciousness. This is why the "small world" the mind lives in, and which we usually perceive, works for us and why we're effortlessly brilliant and yet make the stupidest mistakes.

The mind has, for instance, different levels of working. You can feel these "switches" operating when you listen to people speaking in a foreign language. At first, you don't know what's going on. Then you might identify that the sound you're hearing is not a random noise, or a combination of a couple of people talking inaudibly, or music, or disjointed sounds. It is made up of connected units and is part of a language. Another stage of MOS processing then identifies it as one that you do or don't know. If you've been so trained, all of a sudden your Lithuanian module gets set in place and you're OK. This is why people sometimes have great problems when they know one of two foreign languages that are very similar, as are Spanish and Italian.

The same thing happens when a metaphorical or indirect request is made. First, the sounds outside have to be decoded; E | tz | wah | rm | n | he | er may be first analyzed as to what it means. OK, but what does "It's warm in here" mean, then -- turn down the heat, open the windows or something more romantic? My own work in the analysis of the two sides of the brain comes into play here, where the "low-level" meaning, or decoding the messages from the surroundings, is handled by the left hemisphere, while the interpretation ("it's gonna be a romantic night," *or* "you idiot, why did you light the fireplace so early?") is the province of the right hemisphere.

That the mind serves up the world in all its fullness and complexity is, in truth, the major faith we all share every moment of our lives. But this is a complete misperception based on our insider's point of view -- limited to having one mind, one that writes letters, calculates, smells the meatloaf, and has an "insider's" rather than, say, an engineer's view of what's happening.

That's why psychological science is useful. When we shift the perspective and analysis to the external and scientific, away

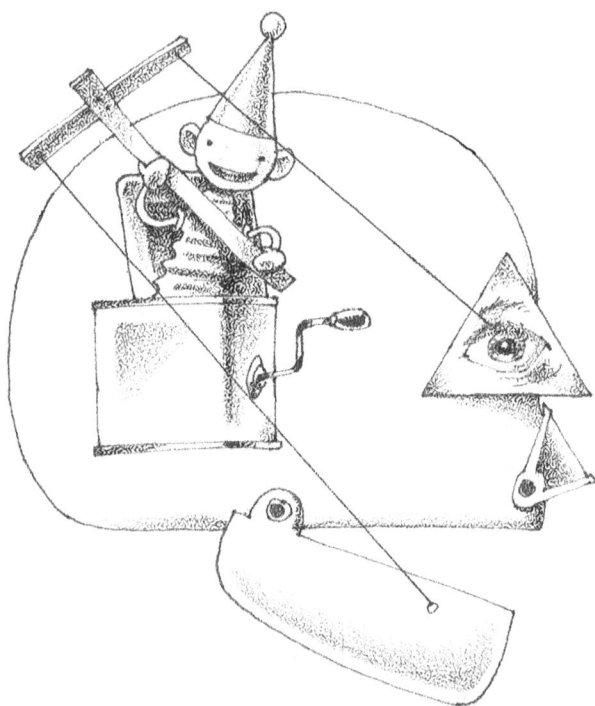

BACKSTAGE

The mental processes that go on backstage to present a view of Reality to you are astounding and end up beguiling you with a totally skewed vision of Reality.

from the personal and particular, the situation inside our heads looks very different. That's the "life of the mind" that this book describes. It consists of an amazingly complex set of processes, all with one aim: to *make things simple for us*. It is a virtual reality produced by a marvelous coordination of tricksters that show us a shell game of a world. We buy into it, because when the mind works in that way, we get through the day, get across the street, get to the meal, get the meaning of the conversation.

That we are experiencing "reality" in its fullness is, too, a belief (although we don't usually discuss it this way) -- one that is stronger, more immediate and pervasive than any religious or cultural ideology. And it is wrong. It is the cause of much misunderstanding about us, about other people, and between societies, companies, even countries.

For most of us, those not schizophrenic or disturbed in some other way, our mundane experience is certainly as dependable as knowing that the sun will rise, go around the earth and set tomorrow. But like the "obvious fact," perceptible to anybody with two eyes and a brain, that the sun goes around the earth (it doesn't), the mind doesn't bring us anything close to reality. It produces a seriously reduced, edited version; in short, a well-crafted illusion. Like the scientific, not personal, knowledge that it is the earth which, in fact, revolves around the sun, the virtual nature of our connection with reality is only understandable from a scientific analysis.

Nobody -- no organism, no plant, no animal, no person -- in truth faces the complete reality that faces us.

Still, in order to be successful, something has to provide any organism -- be it a slug, salmon, turkey, rhesus monkey, graphics hack, internet executive or harassed mother of three -- with a set of alternatives to choose from for the next move. It might be

● ●

WHEN THE WORLD DISAPPEARS

Gaps in the inflow of information from Reality (such as blinking) are covered by MindReal.

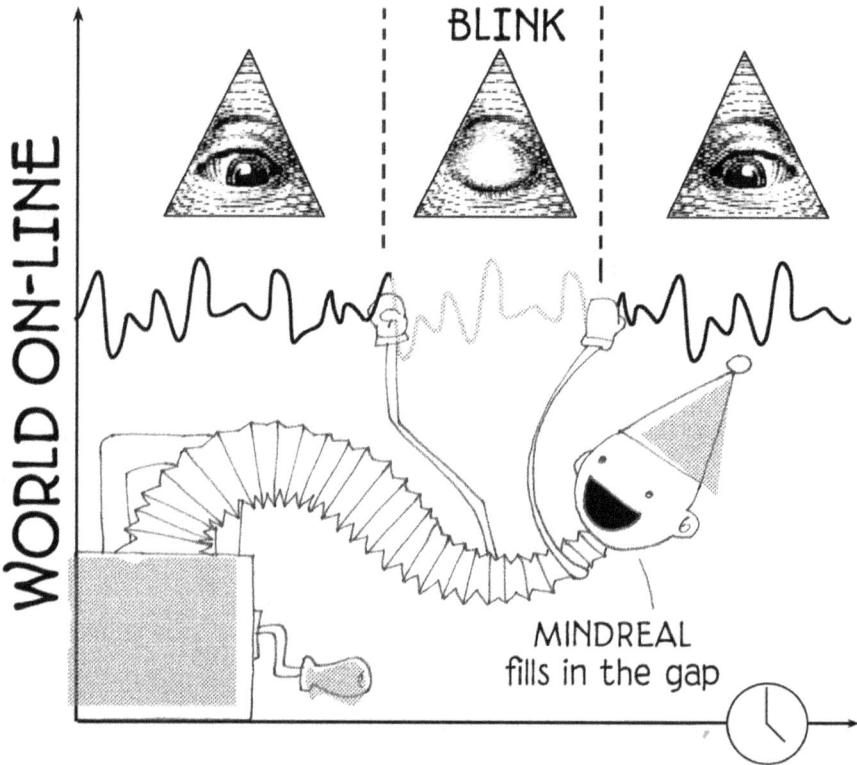

BLINK

WORLD ON-LINE

MINDREAL
fills in the gap

getting food, it might be avoiding a predator, as in the olde days, or it might be, in contemporary life, deciding on a new business venture or a movie to go see. In all cases, the device that provides a shortcut to the action and the world is the mind. But we don't really know much about it, not to mention all of what's happening inside, any more than we are aware of the kidneys removing toxins or, closer to the information world, the complex processes necessary to make a video visible (on a computer) from a digital string of zeros and ones. Our life inside is simple: we just see things, feel them, think them or dream them.

The mind operates "backstage" of consciousness. Mental processes work to present and, really, *re*-present the world of experience; but the mind does so according to its own stealthy set of rules and procedures. These rules are not always what "we'd" like them to be.

Consider this: what day is it? If our memory system were simple, like a date counter on a digital watch, we would be able to answer the question just as quickly on one day as on any other.

Not so. Our memory is not updated, and it is stored only in simplified schemata. If we're asked what day it is on Wednesday, it takes twice as long to answer as when we're asked on Sunday. Weekdays take longer to recall than weekends probably because there are five weekdays and only two weekend days. The closer the weekday is to the weekend, the faster it is recalled. In the real world, the length of every day is equal, but its meaning to us is not. Weekends are perhaps more central to our lives, and therefore we may represent our weeks largely with reference to weekends.[1]

Why doesn't the mind do what "we" want?

First thing to know, and it will seem wacky: you are not your mind.[2]

If the human mind really worked the way "we" wanted it to, why would we say things we didn't wish to, and then regret instantly so doing? Why do we spend $300 on a coffeemaker when we're redoing the house because it seems like nothing; yet a $50 coffeemaker seemed expensive a few weeks earlier? These aren't, in most cases, "mistakes"; they are just evidence of a system at work, one that usually works out, but not always. It goes to the question "who is making these decisions for us, anyway?" So the mind is not *all* of "us"; it is just part of a human being, a part that runs its own show according to its own procedures, just as do the liver and the heart. Clearly, there's another agenda within our heads at work here. Most of what the mind does is secret, taking place out of our awareness and having its own priorities.

The mind, despite the contentions of many academic analyses we often read, isn't like a disembodied computer. It's part of a flesh-and-blood person, and given that, it has a job to do. In a

* *

[1]I've provided many more illustrations in *Multimind, Evolution of Consciousness* and other books.

[2]Of course, there could be all sorts of infernal and interminable discussions then as to who "you" is, but that won't be in this book, you can thank God for that.

word, that job is *survival*. The human mental system evolved to do that job -- to keep the rest of the body out of trouble and to help it find food, safety, shelter, a little lovin' perhaps. These are the priorities that the mind's body needs to survive. They might be as simple as avoiding a car in front of us, as complex as deciding on where to live, as immediate as avoiding food that's poisonous, and as long-range as deciding upon a career. So inside the mind there is an invisible industry, our silent guide to action, preparing responses, organizing information and, mostly, cutting out huge aspects of the world outside of us, so that we can cut through the thicket of information which constantly surrounds us.[3]

Much of what you've learned in school (or if you're young, much of what you'll soon learn) about the mind is often wrong. There are academic distinctions made between perceiving something, remembering an event, imagining the world, and even dreaming; but these are really just ways of describing different events.

Inside the mind, there is not a clear distinction between perceiving something at the moment or long ago. We can't tell, really, what gives rise to our experiences. The same system is in play all the time, and that is why we can misremember or hallucinate

· ·

[3]The academic trend has been to consider mental operations as often consisting of mistakes in judgment, but I think it's better to think of the mind as an adaptive system, though one that isn't completely adapted to every situation, especially in the modern world.

or mix up, just as some do sounds and tastes. Because of a neu-rological anomaly, about one in a thousand people, for instance, can hear colors and taste shapes, as weird as that seems.

So, the usual connections between what's "out there" and what is experienced inside us aren't really fixed. What's in our mind doesn't always depend upon what's happening in front of us all the time.

We can begin close to home to analyze a bit of what goes on every day. Some of it is so obvious, right in front of our eyes, as plain as our nose, and seems at first so banal that, in trying to get through the world, we miss its real significance (READER: bear with me).[4]

If you are like most people, you blink your eyes about nine or ten times each minute, all day, every day. You do so constantly, except when asleep. Think of all this eyelid activity going on: last week you probably blinked close to 50,000 times. Last year, you blinked several million times. Eyes wide shut, again and again. And each time (I'm sure you're noticing the blinks right now!) the world that you see goes away, and we get a tiny bit of black.

But unless your attention is brought to it, you don't really become aware of it during daily activity. What happened to all those mini-blackouts? Why is the complicated visual world un-

· ·

[4]Of course, for most animals, there's no real reason to consider all these psychological complexities. In part that's the point: we're unaware of all the work going on behind the scenes.

interrupted in your experience? What happens to those black moments -- all of them, millions of them -- during a lifetime?

The same thing also happens in front of the eyes and behind the eyes. Remember the standard demonstration of the visual blind spot? At the end of the retina, there are cells that exit the eye to transmit the signals to the visual cortex. All the axons from the eye's ganglion cells leave the eye at the same point, where they are bundled together to form the optic nerve. But these cells, like the terminus of wires in a wall, take up some space. This tiny spot where the ganglion cells exit the eye on the way to the brain is commonly called the "blind spot." There are no photoreceptor cells here, so this part of the eye cannot respond to light. We are not normally aware of the blind spot, because normally we do not see it. But if you try, you can move a small object in front of one of your eyes until it disappears into the blind spot.

So there's a hole in your vision, but you don't see it. And there's more blocking our sight. Blood vessels lie between the retina and the outside of the eye. Because we are structured to respond to changes, we never see these vessels, since they are always there. But you can see for yourself that you do look at the world through blood vessels. Get a penlight, a blank piece of white paper, and a pencil. Turn on the penlight and hold it near the outer edge of your eye and jiggle it around. You will see a luminous red spider web, which is a reflection of the blood vessels. By looking at the paper immediately, you can trace a map of these vessels.

Let's move out of the eye and down just a bit to the nose. If you look ahead carefully, you'll see that the scene in front of you includes your nose. (If you've been gifted with a small nose, then close one of your eyes and you'll see what I mean.) But why didn't you see it before? And in a few moments, your nose will fade away once again, but, once again, why?

So it's immediately obvious that we don't even see what is in front of our eyes when it's there. But the other side of the coin is that we routinely experience events and objects that don't exist. If you write with a pencil that has a rough point, you feel the point as it contacts the paper. This feeling is a cause of much joy; calligraphers love this sensual feel and pick a particular stylus for that special quality.

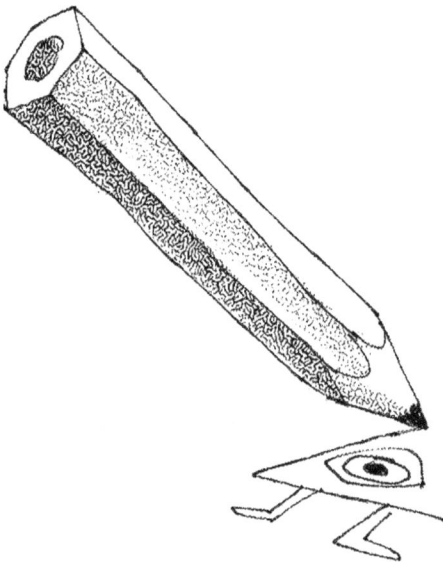

⬤ ⬤

"YOU" ARE HERE?

Your illusory consciousness can do all sorts of tricks, like extending itself into inanimate objects, such as the tip of a pencil.

Feeling the pen as it moves while one is writing is a fairly ordinary experience. But what are you feeling this point *with*? The point isn't, certainly, any part of your body or soul. You're most likely holding the pen an inch or two from the point. There is no part of *you* that is rolling along the paper. You are not feeling anything "real," but you are projecting the feeling forward, out of your hand, into the point. Of course, one could give thousands of other examples, but these will suffice for this short book. It's not a real world we experience, but a set of signals, which we, ourselves, have to learn to shape into a moment-to-moment representation.

As T. S. Eliot said in *Four Quartets*: "We are the music while the music lasts." The experience we have of life is more like connecting the dots in a constellation to form a dipper or a god than it is a solid map of the place. Call this process the building of a virtual shell of a world.

There are extremes of how different the world can be. We see this across cultures, but most dramatically when some people taste shapes, or hear numbers. In *Blue Cats and Chartreuse Kittens* (WH Freeman, 2001), Patricia Duffy gives her experience:

I was sixteen when I found out. The year was 1968. My father and I were in the kitchen, he, in his usual talk-spot by the pantry door, my sixteen-year-old self in a chair by the window. The two of us were reminiscing about the time I was a little girl, learning to write the letters of the alphabet. We remembered that, under his guidance, I'd learned to write all of the letters very quickly except for the letter 'R'.

Until one day I said to my father, "I realized that to make an 'R' all I had to do was first write a 'P' and then draw a line down from its loop. And I was so surprised that I could turn a yellow letter into an orange letter, just by adding a line."

"Yellow letter? Orange Letter?" my father said. "What do you mean?"

"Well, you know," I said. "'P' is a yellow letter, but 'R' is an orange letter. You know -- the colors of the letters."

"The colors of the letters?" my father said.

It had never come up in any conversation before. I had never thought to mention it to anyone. For as long as I could remember, each letter of the alphabet had a different color. Each word had a different color too (generally, the same color as the first letter) and so did each number. The colors of letters, words and numbers were as intrinsic a part of them as their shapes, and like the shapes, the colors never changed. They appeared automatically whenever I saw or thought about letters or words, and I couldn't alter them.

I had taken it for granted that the whole world shared these perceptions with me, so my father's perplexed reaction was totally unexpected. From my point of view, I felt as if I'd made a statement as ordinary as "apples are red" and "leaves are green" and had elicited a thoroughly bewildered response. I didn't know then that seeing such things as yellow 'P's and orange 'R's, or green 'E's, purple '5's, brown 'Mondays' and turquoise 'Thursdays' was unique to the one in two thousand persons like myself who were hosts to a quirky neurological phenomenon called 'synesthesia'. In synesthesia, when one of the five senses is stimulated, both that one plus another sense responds. This can lead 'synesthetes' to experience such peculiarly blended perceptions as words and sounds having colors or even tastes having shapes.

For another synesthete, Michael Watson, the taste of a well-cooked chicken triggered the feeling of holding something pointy in his hand, while an undercooked one triggered the feeling of something disappointingly round. Still another synesthete described the name "Francis" as having "the taste of baked beans."

Since the mind is so complex, I am going to switch metaphors around in this book, because I don't want anybody to think I've reduced the mind to a computer or a mirrored funhouse or the like. So for the moment, think of the mind as an elaborate set of cat's whiskers, antennae that touch parts of the world so that the cat can navigate. Each organism selects and elaborates what it needs in order to get through the day in its neighborhood. If you are a plant, you don't need to know much; if you are a frog, a few items reach the sensorium; a cat more; a bonobo much more; and we, hopefully, more still.

Virtual and different, but the "shells" are not completely imaginary, either. The "reality" we live inside -- for us, for ants, cows, even grass, for all I know -- is a virtual one. This "illusion" that we live inside is compelled by our circumstances and limited by the information-processing machinery that we and other organisms have.

By that I mean we can't have just any old illusion of what's happening, or we'll walk into busses or tigers would have eaten our ancestors. So the mind's shell has to represent important events in the outside world well enough so we can avoid them or eat them or see them or reproduce with them, and so we can be successful.

There is a poem, popular in the '60s, written by Lawrence Ferlinghetti called "A Coney Island of the Mind." I'd think, now, of the virtual reality we live inside as a "Las Vegas of the mind." A mirage that functions. Things are placed there and stuck together whether they exist or not.

Much that does exist, like the arid desert in Las Vegas, is ignored, and things that do not exist, like the touch at the end of the pencil (or the Eiffel Tower in the middle of a desert), do appear. Old memories coexist with new experiences; thoughts from a few days ago are still around, mingling with the sounds of a current conversation; dreams can take it all over, not only when we're asleep, but sometimes while we're awake as well. I wrote in *Multimind* that stuck side-by-side, inside the skin, inside the skull, are several special-purpose, separate, specific small minds.

● ●

"YOU" ARE NOT YOUR MIND

Your consciousness is an illusion that hovers above the multitude of shifting mental processes that grind on beneath our awareness.

The mind isn't well-designed, though; it's just accumulated. The particular collection of talents, abilities and capacities that each person possesses depends upon a lot of things. It depends partly on birth and partly on experience. Our illusion, however, is that somehow we are unified, that all our actions, or at least many of them, do have a common purpose and goal.

We have a rolling virtual resumé of ourselves that we find quite easy to generate. "I'm a successful executive with a home in the hills and enjoy vacations by the water." "I'm a basketball fan and the second son of a drunk." Other people, as well, present a smooth, seemingly consistent and unified surface to us. But that idea we have of ourselves and of other people is construction -- just as much as is seeing a tree outside is constructed on a limited basis. We are hidden from ourselves, and while the skin covers a lot of different organs that are only visible once the covering has been lifted, it is more difficult, of course, to blow the lid off the mind.

But the mind is a mixed structure; it has modules and what I call policies within it. In life, these general components act independently of one another and may very well have vastly different priorities. The mind is not an organized system, but a squadron of simpletons. It is not unified, not rational, not well designed or even designed at all. In fact, although it is difficult for us to face, the mind simply happened. It was propagated through the innovations of countless organisms that lived long before us, and the mind evolved, not through design, but through countless animals and through countless worlds.

Like the rest of biological evolution, the human mind is a collage of adaptations -- the propensity to do the right thing in a certain situation, to drink, to return home to one's place of birth, to be able to navigate using the stars. Our thought is a set of fixed routines, "simpletons." We need them; it is vital to be able to find the right food at the right time; it is vital to be able to mate well, to generate children, to avoid marauders, to respond quickly to emergencies. And countless mental routines to handle all of this housekeeping work evolved over millions of years and developed in different eras.

Thus, to characterize the mind as primarily rational, as much scientific analysis has it, is an injustice. It sells us short; it makes us misunderstand ourselves and has perverted our understanding of our intelligence, our schooling, and our physical and mental health.*

Holding up rationality and remorseless deliberation as the mind's primary function has, more importantly, set us along the wrong road to our future. Instead of being the pinnacle, rationality is just one small peak in a range of enormous possibilities. Because human beings live all over the world, from the Himalayas to the Kalahari to Paris, the human mind evolved great breadth; yet it is shallow, for it creates quick-and-dirty "sketches" of the world. This rough-and-ready sketchy reality enabled our ancestors to survive better, and that's why the mind evolved -- not so that we could know ourselves. The mind didn't evolve for self-knowledge.

*This is based on a discussion in my *The Evolution of Consciousness*.

Simply speaking, there has never been, nor will there ever be, enough time to be truly rational. Rationality is used rarely and in a very limited area. It is not practical, anyway. There is no time for the mind to go through the luxurious exercise of examining alternatives.

Instead of the standard rational analysis of evidence which involves setting up a "truth table" -- a checklist of information about whether propositions are correct or are not to know -- you're aware that you already know a lot of things. You know that Zurich is in Switzerland, you know that New York is in America, etc. But, to know what Moses' phone number was, you would have to go through a "truth table" involving an immense set of calculations and information searches, if you didn't already know that there weren't phones in Moses' time -- shortcuts.

Think of the number of issues you immediately know accurately -- what England is, whether you would ride a skateboard to a formal dinner, whether the chicken goes on the inside or the outside of the sandwich, what your spouse wore this morning -- and you will see that your own truth table, if entered randomly, would have to contain millions of entries. And how much time would it take to search? Years! When a tiger approached, imagine an animal that deliberated this long and thought, "Is this thing friendly? What is this expansive yellow in my visual field? Look at those neat ears and deep eyes... Hey, look at those teeth!" We can say, from a technical standpoint, that such an organism would not have been around long enough to contribute its genes to future generations. So, obviously, rationality and remorseless deliberation are too slow in real life, although fine for academic or scientific work.

The mind is one great shortcut, for better or worse. We don't search out all the alternatives in an attempt for knowledge. Instead, we use very, very few simple strategies. The mind works overwhelmingly in large part to act -- to do or die, as we say in English -- but not to reason or to know why. Most of our little routines are automatic moves; not so automatic, perhaps, as re-

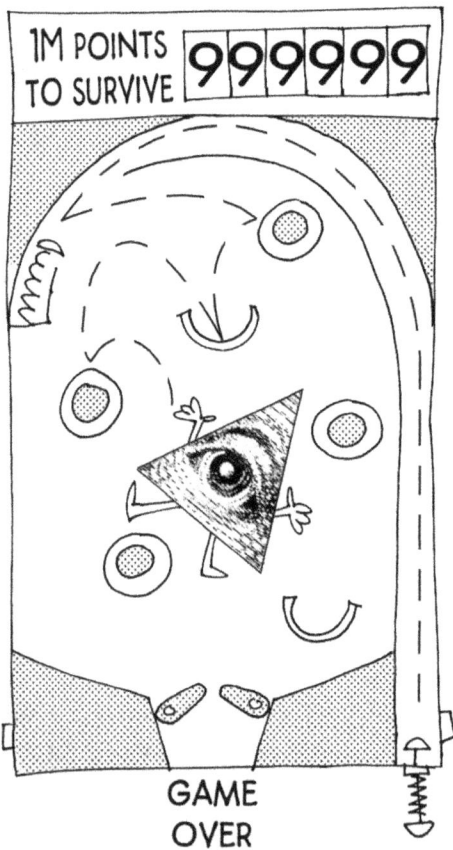

· ·

1M POINTS
TO SURVIVE 999999

GAME
OVER

MIND BOGGLING

Consciousness is bounced around helplessly by environmental influences. We are usually unaware of the turmoil that consciousness is subjected to by the world outside our heads. The irony is that this system was, like all evolved systems, a direct result of natural selection.

moving one's hand from a hot stove, but stored and fixed routines, like military exercises.

The primary job of the mental system is not self-understanding, self-analysis or reason, but rather running its routines. That is what the mind is organized to do; it runs its routines to adapt to the world, to get nourishment and safety, to reproduce and so to pass on descendants. The human mind evolved thus a fantastic and alluring set of adaptations within which to operate and to mesh with the small world, the local environment in which each of us finds us. The mind works to gain a quick fix on reality and to guide action.

But the mind isn't any one thing. Like an army, it has its master builders, its accountants, its dullards, its stooges, its hysterical spirits, and, especially, its dreamers. The mind contains separate and independent streams of thinking, feeling and ideas, and these transfer from one situation into another. Sigmund Freud elaborated on an important mental routine in his analysis of what was called "transference," which involves the projection of the patient's own feelings toward significant others onto the psychotherapist. But transference isn't limited to the therapeutic encounter. In fact, minds come into consciousness and transfer reactions all the time. This swapping of reactions leaves our consciousness unaware of how a new and different mind is in place for determining our reactions.

We can use the concept of "mind in place" to show how we recruit the same routines to handle different situations. Picture different "sets of mind" swinging in and out, while one system, then another, then a third takes hold of consciousness. Once recruited for a purpose, the mind in place performs as if it had been there forever. Then it steps aside, to be replaced with another actor, one with different memories, different priorities and plans; and we, our conscious self, rarely notice what's gone on.

And one consequence of this is that we are not the same person from moment to moment. Thus, the idea most people have that they are consistent is an illusion caused by the structure of the mind. It is simply that the "observer" part of the mind also has quite limited access to what is going on. The "self" is itself just another part of the mind, nothing special and with a small job. And that job isn't self-knowledge, rationality or understanding, but rather it is what you might call "minding the store."

And the situation is even more complicated as an engineering task: the world, this world we're describing, is but one-trillionth of the total energy that strikes us. There is a thicket of information out there that we miss constantly: infrared, ultraviolet, waves that birds hear, and the like. All that we're describing here is already so reduced by what Aldous Huxley called the "reducing valve" of the senses that we hardly experience anything of what's "out there." It's all in our heads, much more than we think. How many leaves have you seen this summer?

And one more bullet before we move on: The mind is, really, not identical with the brain. Surely the mind depends on the brain, and some people (even the writer of this book) have made a career of writing about the functions of the two sides of the brain and the mind. But the mind has a status independent of the brain. To greatly, but not completely, oversimplify: the brain's workings can be visualized better as if it were a corporation's organizational chart where the physical location and appearance of the CEO (the mind) may not matter much. Also, as anybody who works knows, the real influence and intrigue of an organization are not possible to comprehend from its physical arrangement.

And there are more complications to the simple ("get me through the day") role that the mind has. If you think about it, there's too much information available -- we don't face reality so much as we *de*face it, taking only small parts and creating or filling in the gaps to help us through the day. Then, it has to be put together again. First, the world is split into senses, for example, and we make the same (seemingly from this perspective) dumb mistakes over and over, because we never "see" things whole. Ordinarily, no matter how self-reflective we are, we don't know what the mind is doing or how it does it.

We know what is on our mind, because we see, feel, think, hear and taste objects and events, but we don't know what's *in* our mind because we can't see it. The structure of our mental system and our consciousness is invisible and imperceptible to us. Nevertheless, which "DJ" is in place in the mind determines how we decide who to marry, what to spend and to do at any moment, the content of our memories, which strategies we use to think and, in the long run, the future of how humanity handles Earth.

But it may be easier than we think if the world we see is really something we each construct on our own, because thus we can change it. By the way, after you've read this analysis, you may well think it a miracle that a human being can find anything in

the outside world, or get anything to eat, or find shelter or somebody to mate with. And it *is* a miracle, this life of the mind. And
understanding these daily miracles -- that's what this book is
about.

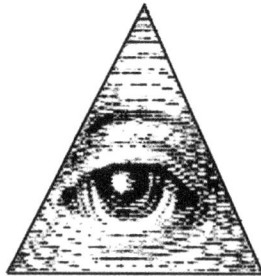

WHO'S PLAYING THE TUNES?

Much of what goes on in our minds is determined by imperceptible and invisible policies. Which "DJ" is in place in the mind is usually out of our conscious control.

Man, these tunes are totally *MindReal*!

bang
bang
bang

THE
MindReal
TOUR

··

MAKING
MindReal

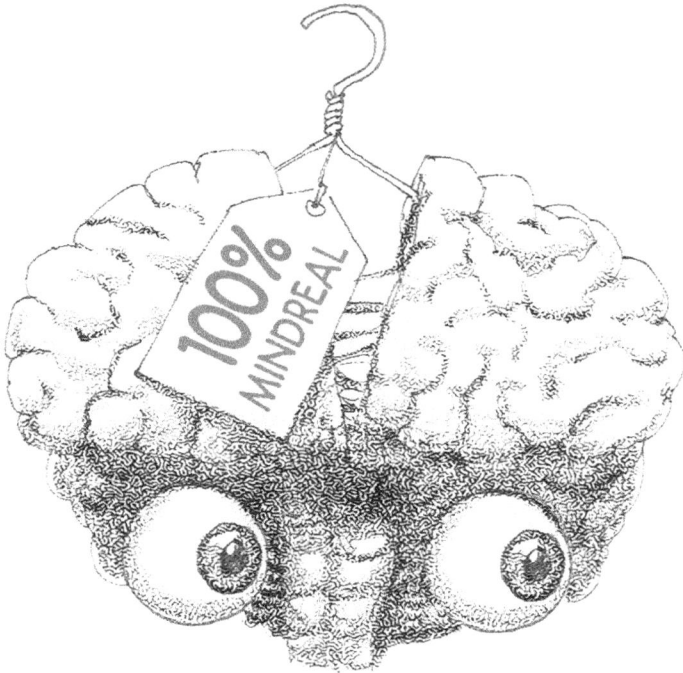

I can't believe Mind LTD **creates** such a convincing illusion.

Crazy, isn't it? You hang the great *edifice* of MindReal on the thinnest filtered and processed strand of Reality imaginable.

The other thing that will surprise you is how much *time* it takes Mind LTD to **create** MindReal. First, consider the time it takes for the brain's neurons to fire and react to stimuli, both from Reality and from the body and brain itself...

I'm *firing*! Pass on the message, you two!

OK, OK, we got the message...

Oi, what does it all *mean*, anyhow?

Let someone *else* deal with what it all means. Hey, *listen* up! Here come *more* stimuli!

Then there's all the time that the *pig-headed workers* of Mind LTD need to do their bit. They need to be *managed* as well. They have to make very quick decisions about how to interpret the reduced strand of signals from the neurons. All this has to happen *before* MindReal is presented to you.

So what's happening to *me* while they're busy doing all this *work* to make *MindReal*?

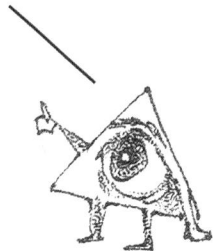

All this only takes a *half-second* to deal with-- sometimes even quicker. It's fabulously effective. The only downside is that you get *confused* now and then between *Reality* and *MindReal.* You see "red" and believe that "red" is somehow really out there; but, of course, the color red is just a product of Mind LTD, based on some filtered information it's received from Reality. MindReal is a *virtual fairy tale.* Colors, sounds, sensations--all of it one big lie created to keep you oriented and alert to *danger* and *opportunity.*

DANGER

WARINESS

OPPORTUNITY

WAIT ½ SEC

What's *really* strange is that you don't even *notice* the half-second delay! Mind LTD *fools* you into thinking that the action took place half-a-second *before* they deliver the current version of MindReal. It's like they somehow put a fake *early date* on the postmark.

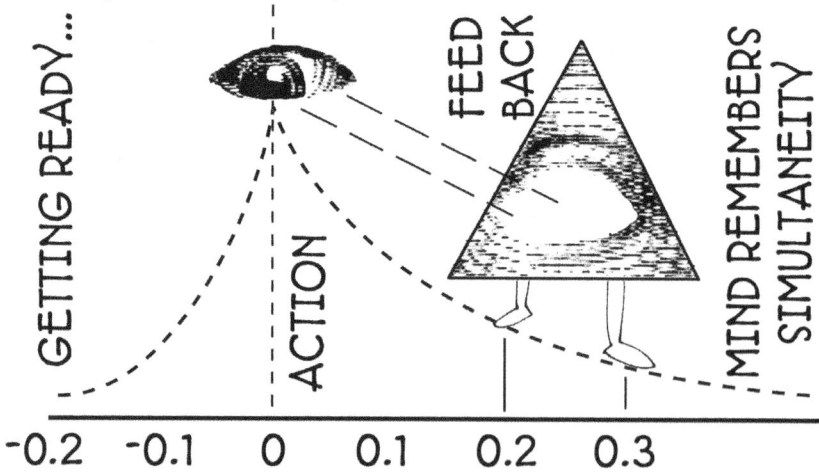

GETTING READY... ACTION FEED BACK MIND REMEMBERS SIMULTANEITY

-0.2   -0.1   0   0.1   0.2   0.3

Oddly enough, even now that I've told you about MindReal, you *really can't tell* that Mind LTD is making it all up. Of course, **some** sort of Reality really does exist out there, but that's not what Mind LTD **"sees."** Some people think that Reality is an illusion, but that's not the case. *MindReal* is the illusion; it's just that you confuse MindReal with Reality.

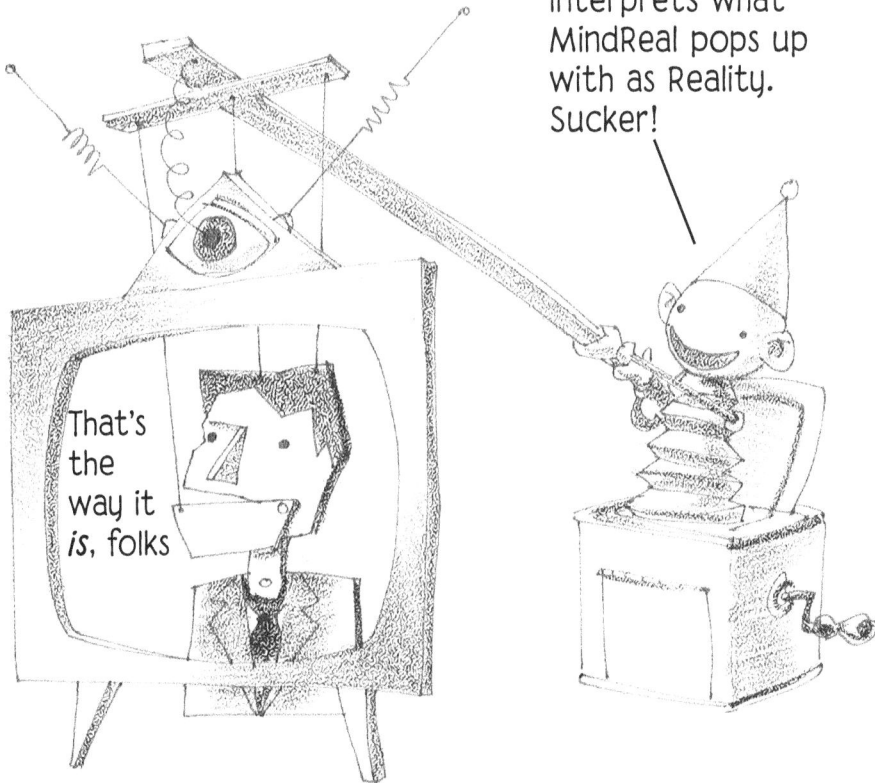

It's just so hard to *accept* all this....

Consciousness interprets what MindReal pops up with as Reality. Sucker!

That's the way it *is*, folks

Mind LTD doesn't even realize that it's not coping with the world very well, until **consciousness** takes notice of its mistakes. This happens when **you** say, "why did I do that? I must be an *idiot*."

Oh yeah, I say that all the time. I just thought maybe I was *stupid* or something.

No, you're **not** stupid. Sometimes you even wake up to the consequences of *abusing* a tool that was created for a *totally* different job. Mind LTD was *never designed* to tackle the modern world, just like a screwdriver was never designed to be used as a *hammer*.

That won't stop me *trying*.

Every once in awhile you might get a *glimpse* of the time it takes for Mind LTD to sort itself out.

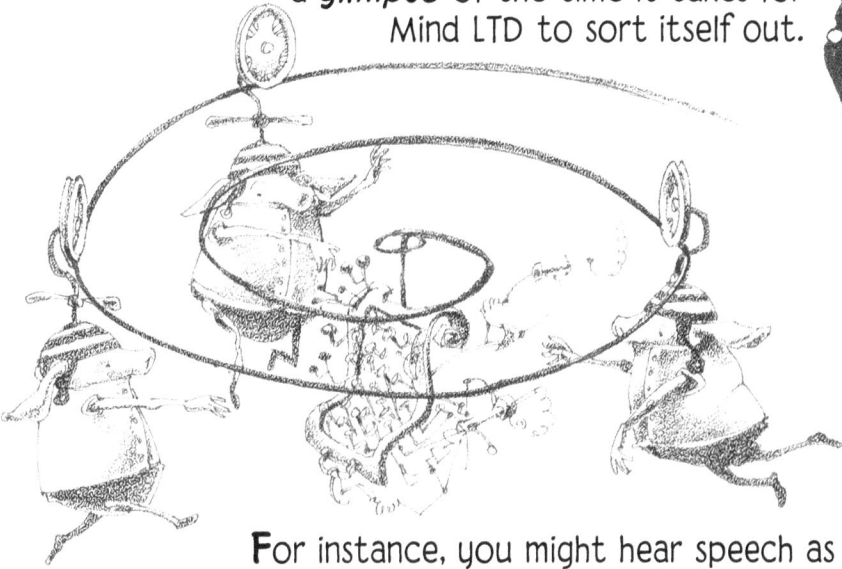

For instance, you might hear speech as *incomprehensible sounds* for a few seconds, until that particular language is *identified* and then finally *understood.*

"qui j'ècoute?"

Hmm...those sounds are *weird*...can't *figure out* what's being said.

Waitaminit...ah! It's *French!* Here, you handle *this* one, *Frenchler.*

Pas de problème. C'est *moi, ici!*

This'll keep him fooled.
Ha Ha!

Don't underestimate the **power** of Mind LTD to create a very **convincing** MindReal. These guys have been training for **eons!**

Goodness...and all this time I thought *I* was the boss...

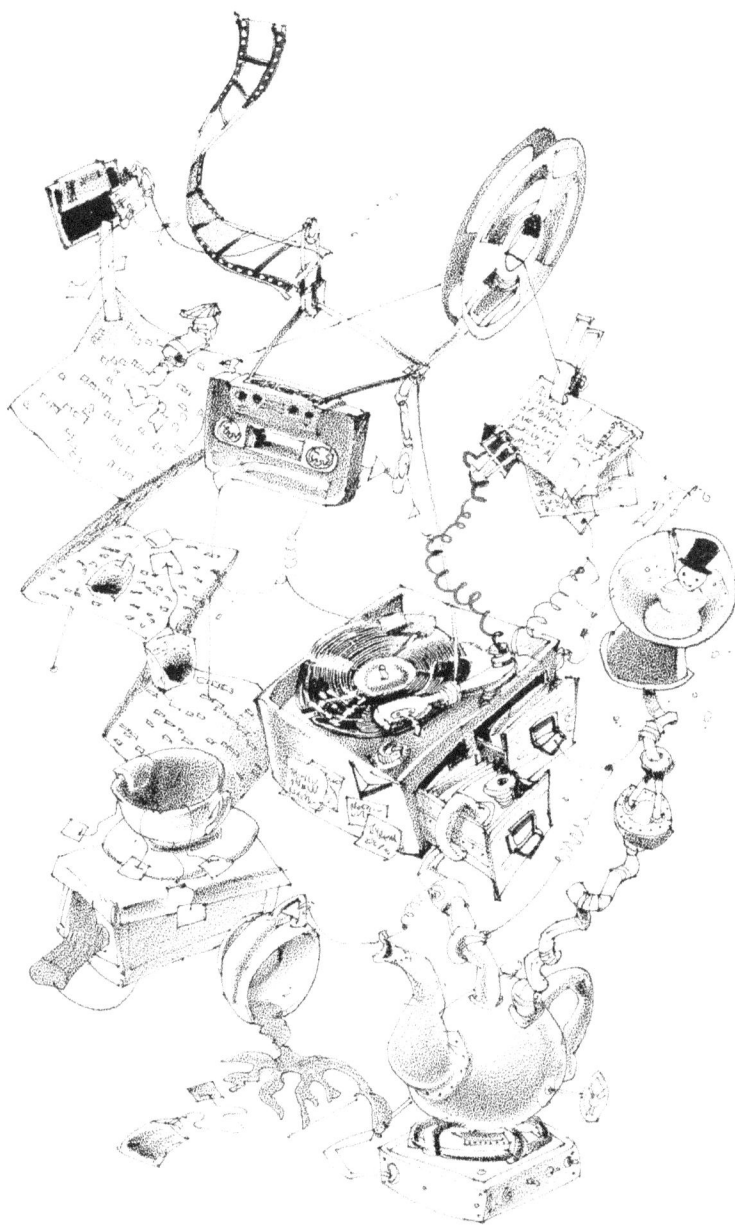

Between the acting of a dreadful thing
And the first motion, all the interim is
Like a phantasma, or a hideous dream.
The Genius and the mortal instruments
Are then in counsil, and the state of man,
Like to a little kingdom, suffers then
The nature of an insurrection.

-- *William Shakespeare*, Julius Caesar

2

• •

THE TIME TO CREATE THE MIND'S REALITY

OUR EXPERIENCE OF THE WORLD IS DELAYED ABOUT HALF A SECOND (!)

When we become aware of an event in the world around us, it's obvious that we do so as it happens. However, there's new evidence that we may not actually see things when they happen. Benjamin Libet studied neurological patients who had electrodes implanted in their cortices for therapeutic purposes.[1] By applying direct electrical stimulation to the somato-sensory cortex, which is responsible for conscious perception of touch, he was able to cause the subject to feel a nearly natural

[1]There is no pain in the brain so no anesthetic is needed, and it is very useful for the patient to remain conscious so he or she can describe the results of stimulation.

sensation near the wrist. He found that the electrical impulses to the brain had to last about 500 milliseconds (ms) before the subject became aware of the sensation. In civilian terms, that's half a second!

He then gave subjects a very short electrical stimulus to their wrists 200 ms after initiating a 500-ms-long cortical stimulus. He expected that in each case there would be a 500-ms delay before the patient felt the stimuli, and that since the cortical stimulus came first, it would be felt first. However, the subjects felt the sensation from the skin stimulus before the one resulting from cortical stimulation. Since they had reported no awareness of cortical stimuli less than 500 ms long, the skin stimulus must have been processed in another way. Libet then applied the brain stimulus to neuronal pathways before they reached the cortex. This time he found that the subjects perceived the skin stimulus at the same time as the stimulus to the brain.

What difference does it make to the brain if the stimulus begins at the skin, before the cortex (subcortically), or at the cortex? Both skin stimulation and subcortical stimulation produce what brain scientists call a primary-evoked response -- a spike of neuronal activity in the area of the cortex devoted to outside stimulation. Stimulation directed at the cortex does not produce this response.

Given the half-second required for a direct-brain stimulus to reach awareness, why does it take almost no time to feel an electrical pulse at the wrist?

Remember our discussion of feeling the tip of a pencil as it writes over a page -- a situation in which there could be no actual stimulus, but something we make up to cover? Here, Libet's conclusion is that when the skin stimuli were strong enough to be consciously felt, the brain somehow referred the experience back to the time that it actually occurred, using the *start* of the evoked response as a marker. The delay required between a stimulus and the attainment of neuronal adequacy may provide a time in which perceptions could be modified or excluded from consciousness. This could be a mechanism for repressing unwanted perceptions, something like the 5-second delay, known as a Broadcast Delay, used by radio and television stations to catch and bleep undesirable speech or actions.

The lag between information and awareness could serve as a filter to prevent too much information from entering consciousness. And the referral back in time would allow this "brain delay" to occur without putting us a half-second out of synchrony with the world. The delay between the occurrence of events and the brain's response may mean that any fast (less than 500 ms) responses to events that are processed in this way must happen before the stimulus reaches conscious levels. Thus, we may react to many things we are not even conscious of.

And how does the conscious self know what is going on in the head?

It doesn't.

It seems to work on a "just say no" basis, as Shakespeare described.

Again, we rely on Libet, who examined patients who were undergoing open-head surgery. This allowed him to record from different areas of the brain while the patients were awake. He asked the patients to tell him when they were going to do something. He compared the readiness potential (particular brainwaves) that precedes an act with the patient's report of the subjective experience of wanting to act. For example, if the subject is asked to prepare to move at a certain time, the readiness potential appears; and when he is asked to prepare to move but to veto the move just before the time, the readiness potential also appears.

These experiments imply that before an intention to act reaches consciousness, it has *already* triggered processes in the brain. Thus, much of our behavior may arise unconsciously. However, the ability of the subject to veto the intention to act after the unconscious process had begun indicates that we may have some kind of retroactive control of our behavior -- but only if we are aware that an intention to act has been triggered. One function of consciousness may be to veto spontaneous plans, even if those plans are made within our own brain. When differences in plans or information produce contradictory interpretations of experience, consciousness provides us with a unique, consistent interpretation. We see only one interpretation of a Necker cube at a time.

That doesn't mean that our working in the world itself is out of synch; but, like the pencil example, our moment-to-moment experience is in some cases "referred" back in time, and in all cases is assembled like memories from the information available.

It's good enough most of the time, but sometimes, like updating memory, our experience has to be revised quickly.

These findings have, however, been the cause of philosophical and popular hyperspeculation and discussion, since most people don't understand our central point, which is: our experience is virtual. Believing something else, some writers have tried to

READINESS POTENTIAL

Before an intention to act reaches consciousness, it has already triggered measurable processes in the brain.

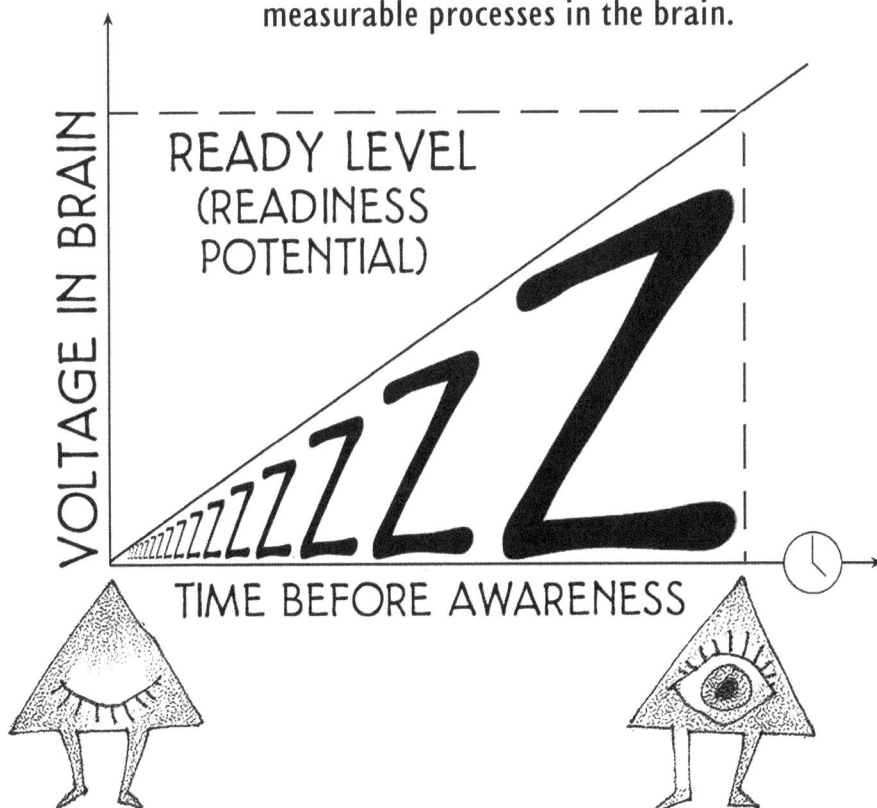

READY LEVEL (READINESS POTENTIAL)

VOLTAGE IN BRAIN

TIME BEFORE AWARENESS

draw religious and spiritual conclusions from the "just say no" functions of consciousness. Here, a simple organizing principle -- logical, really, given the confusion inside -- somehow becomes a basis for changes in Judeo-Christian morality. See, for instance, Nørretrander's otherwise very useful *The User Illusion*.[2]

Libet himself sees a threat to our normal philosophy: "That one's consciousness might lag behind the brain processes that control one's body seems, to some, an unsettling and even depressing prospect, ruling out a real (as opposed to illusory) 'executive role' for 'the conscious self'. . . a dissociation between the timings of the corresponding 'mental' and 'physical' events would seem to raise serious though not insurmountable difficulties for the . . . theory of psychoneural identity."

But there need not be a threat; this is just a complicated confusion. The mind makes itself up and produces a virtual reality from its information. It's not correct at any time, but it is good enough, as we said, to get through the day. There are so many other holes in the mind -- the blind spot, sensing events by their change rather than their absolute -- that being behind the times, all the time, is just another part of the virtual reality that we need to produce.

[2]A particularly elaborate and mistaken discussion is to be found in Dennett, D.C. & Kinsbourne, M. (1995), "Time and the observer: The where and when of consciousness in the brain." *Behavioral and Brain Sciences* 15 (2): 183-247.

It would, even with our brains, have to take some time to assemble, no?

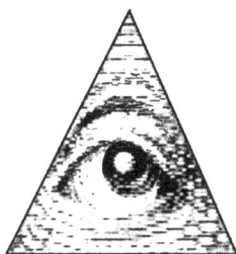

• • •

THE
MindReal
TOUR
...

MANAGING
MindReal

THIS IS A
**THINKING-
CAP AREA**

CAPS MUST BE
WORN AT
ALL TIMES

Like it or not, here's the **company of pig-headed mind workers** that evolution has left you with. Things don't always go smoothly, but then what do you expect from a ramshackle and disorganized ad-hoc bunch?

Is someone behind us?

Some pig-heads handle **language**, some handle **memory**, some tie things **together**, others take things **apart**. Some group together to form special **"talent forces"** to handle specific skills that need a **combination** of workers.

What's for lunch?

Different workers are automatically *wheeled in* by associations, physiology and memories to perform their *mental alchemy.*

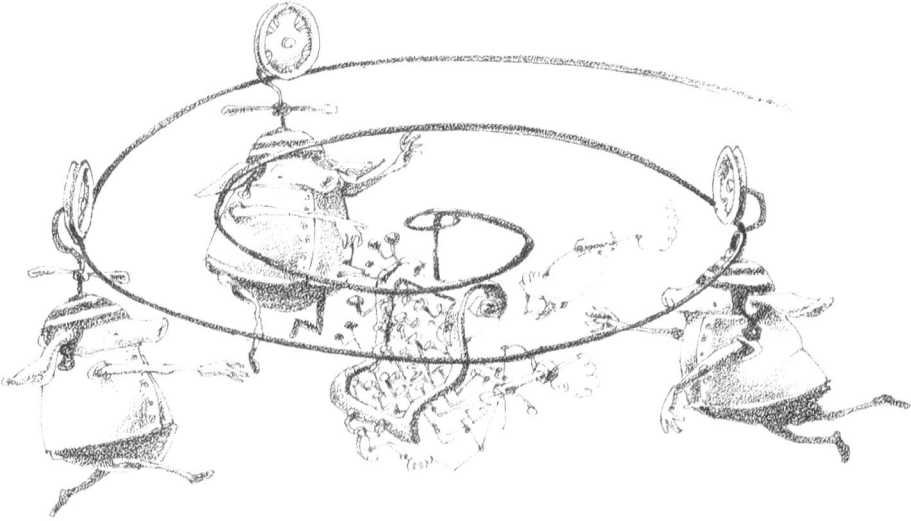

So *who's managing* all this *wheeling* of my pig-heads?

That's a *problem.* Nobody is really in *charge* of the way these guys work. Not even *you* realize how little control you have over *which* pig-heads get wheeled in. Pig-head staffing is mainly influenced by what's going on in the *outside* world. That's why Mind LTD is so *easily manipulated*.

Lessee...sticks,
right angles...
coupla *diagonals*...

Got it--cube...
right, what's next?

They're pretty
good at settling
on the *simplest*
interpretation
of what they're
confronted with.

But once *Mind LTD workers* settle on an
interpretation, it's nearly *impossible* to
reinterpret. For example, once the *pig-
heads* have decided that this bunch of
rippled lines below indicates a bumpy
surface...

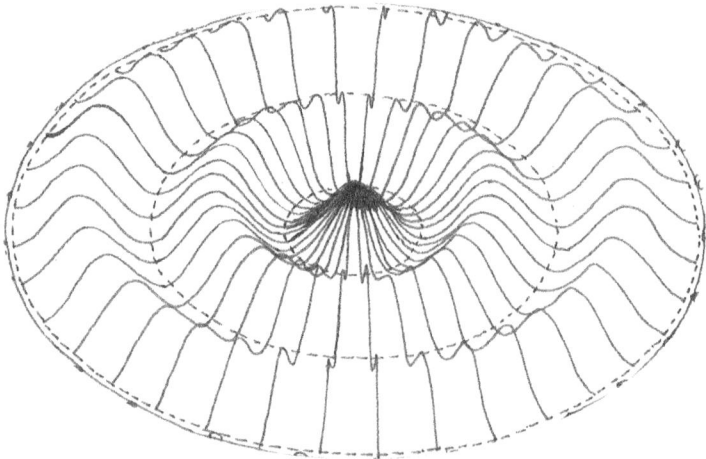

...you'll have a hell of a time trying to see them for what they are in reality: a bunch of ripply lines on a flat piece of paper! This is a good example of just how powerful MindReal is, even when you know in reality that the drawing is flat. Mind LTD has created a 3-D object for you!

Aarrgh! You're right! I *know* this is just a drawing, but I keep seeing it as a *3-D shape.* No matter how I try, I just *can't flatten* it!

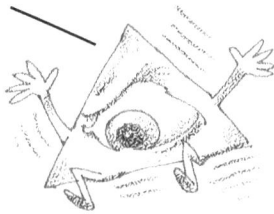

boing!
boing!
BOING!

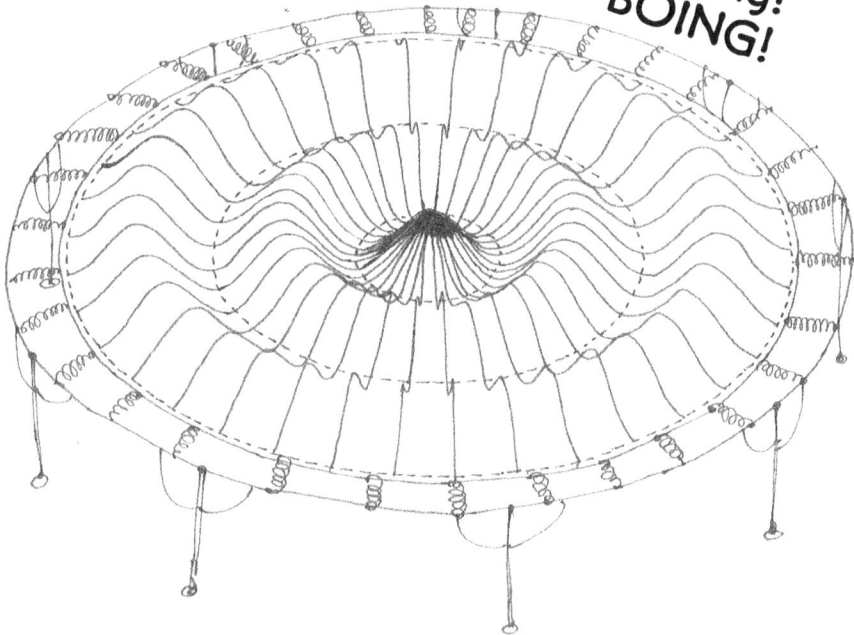

You're so easily *duped* into *believing* your own hallucinations, and you're *blind* to some things as obvious as the *nose on your face.*

Come off it-- like *what?*

Well, how about the *nose on your face?*

Oh, yeah, there it is...I *forgot* about that...I see it *now*, though!

Of course when I *point it out* to you, you notice your nose.

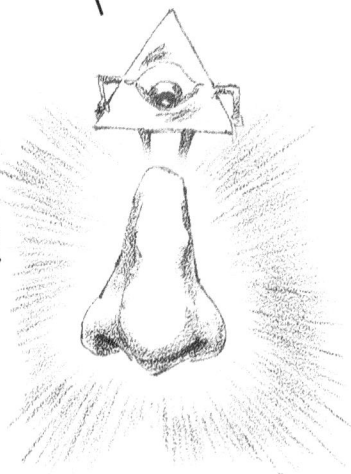

What's more, these pig-headed workers are total *suckers* for whatever hasty mistakes they make. Watch what this pig-head makes of these three black circles with a chunk taken out.

HEY, there's a triangle there!

Uh, yeah, I can see what you're talking about, but it's not really there, is it?

Whadya mean? Can't you *see* it? Look, stupid, *Triangle!* **Triangle!**

Try as you might, you'll be hard-pressed to convince the little pig-head otherwise. He's made his decision.

MINDREAL is most vivid in young children who often are in a *dream-like world.* They haven't had enough *experience* with Reality to know what to expect, and so *anything goes*, especially when it's *dark*!!

That's why it's sometimes easier to fall in love with a *vague* person than a person with a strong personality. People with strong personalities leave less to your imagination, whereas vague people are better *canvases* for you to project your *own fantasies* onto.

You think, therefore **I am** your own true love

It can get pretty *scary* when *MindReal* starts *speaking* in **my voice!**

EEEK!

GOD SAYS: KILL FAMOUS PERSON.

STALE CUPCAKE THROWN FROM WINDOW OF NEARBY BUILDING

In places where people are *regularly bombarded* with *alien visitation* stories, *MindReal* is *primed* to turn every flash in the sky into an *alien spaceship.*

Hey, what's that *flying* object?

Dunno, I can't *identify* it.

That makes it an *unidentified flying object!* A UFO!

ALIEN INVASION! RUN FOR YOUR LIVES!

Mind LTD is subject to *prejudice*...after all, it was once necessary for survival to cast *instant judgment* upon strangers. Those who were able to decide quickly whether a stranger was *friend* or *foe* survived, while the more thoughtful ones may have been killed off by their foes while they were dithering.

Generalizations turned out to be handy for judging the character of others. So if one member of a rival tribe was your *enemy*, then Mind LTD assumed that the rest would be enemies as well. Evolution selected for *racism!* The mind is all wired up to *pigeon-hole* people.

What a *bird-brained* scheme *that* is!

PISCES JEW

BLACK TEXAN

HOUSEWIFE PROPHET

My goodness, that causes so much *trouble* and *destruction*, doesn't it.

What's the buzz?

What's new pussycat?

Don't go beating around the bush!

What's that *awful song* those pig-heads are listening to?

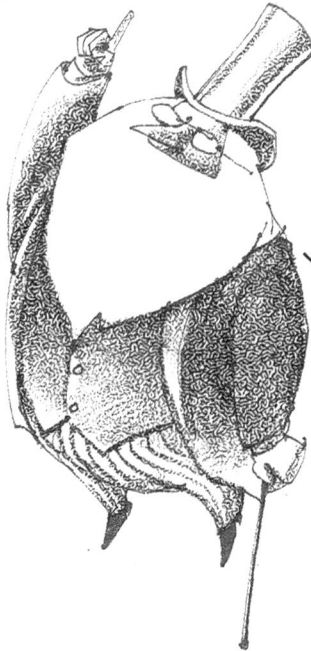

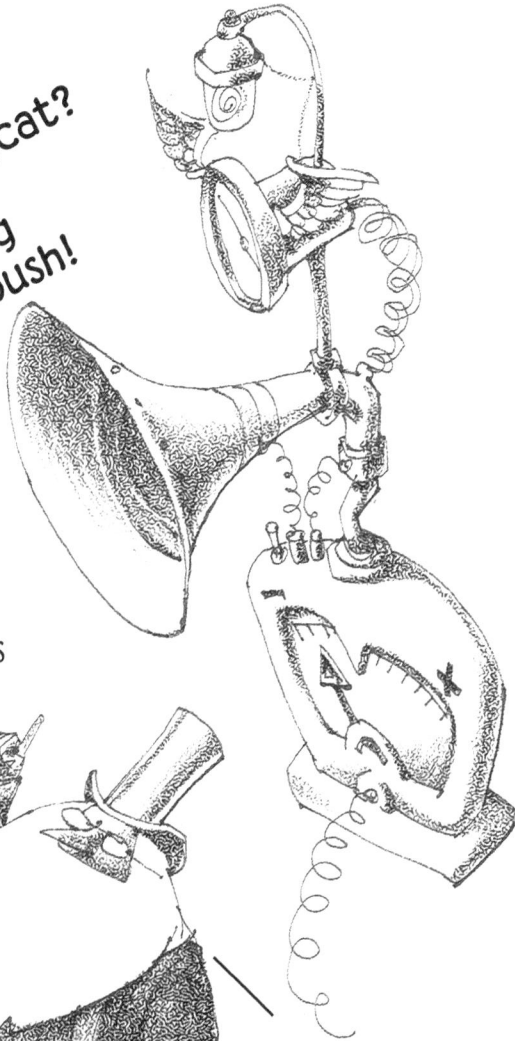

That's the *perpetual tape-loop* of Mind LTD's *policies.* It's sort of the *company psych-song.*

It's so **stupid and annoying**...doesn't it affect the way they work?

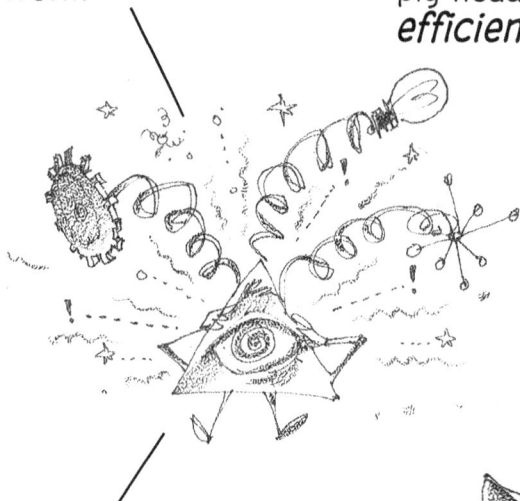

Precisely. But it turns out that having the infernal propaganda broadcast at all times makes these pig-headed characters work more **efficiently.**

It's driving me **nuts!**

If anyone **ever** turned that music off, we'd all be **dead**, pal. We'd forget how to act **quickly and simply.** Now, lemme see, what was I doing just then...

Of course, it's not just *Reality* that gets treated like this. *Memories* as well must be woven together from the thinnest strands and recreated each and every time they're called up.

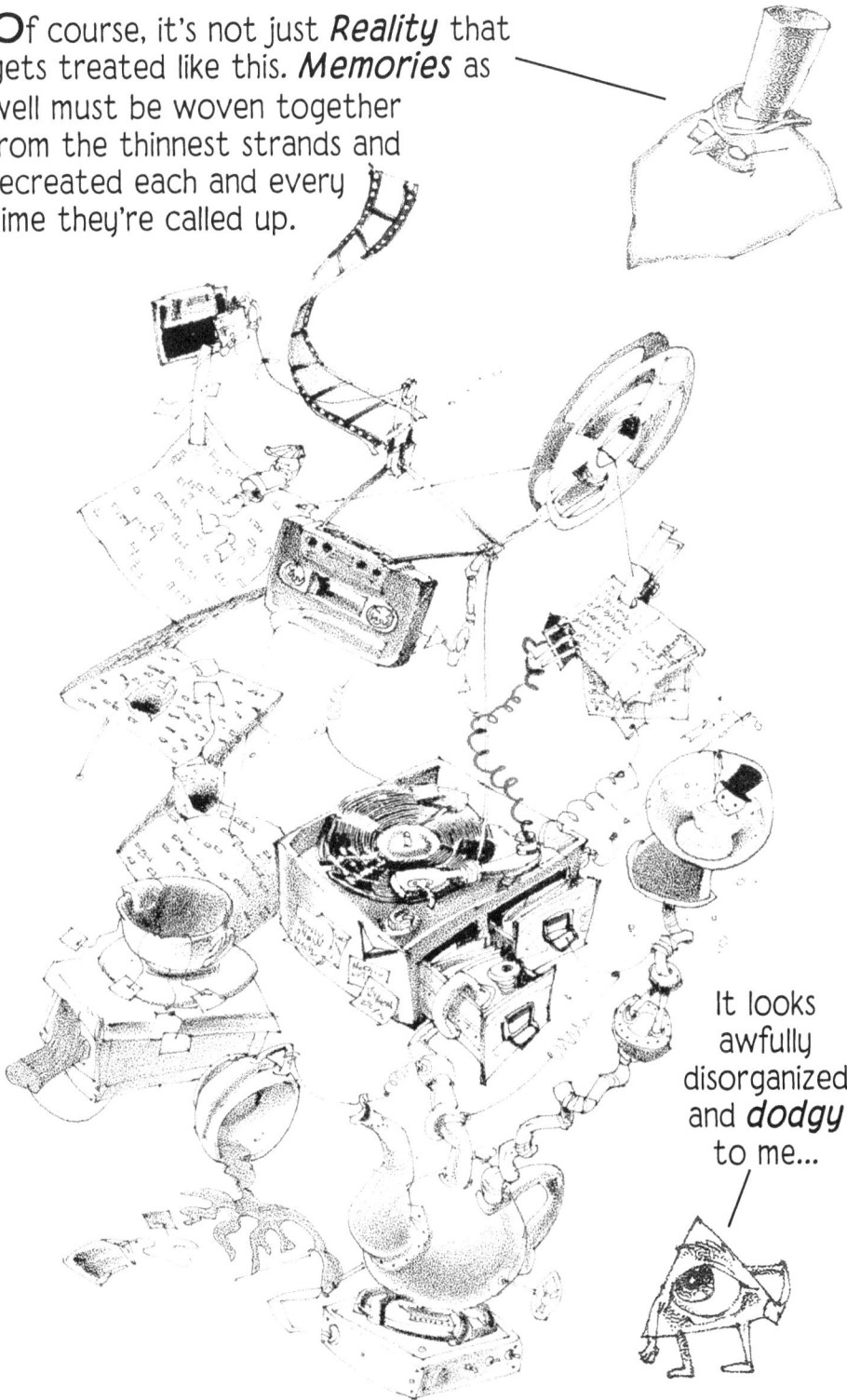

It looks awfully disorganized and *dodgy* to me...

Yo! We got a request for *Christmas Day, 1979*--can you remix for us?

We'll do our *best*...

Far from being anything like computer memory, *human memories* are reassembled and combined and corrupted with bits of the present.

Now, what did Auntie Beth *look like* back then?

This is what she looks like now... *WHOOPS*, doggone, now where did that *old image go*?

Aw *heck*, this will do...

Good God! They're totally mangling that memory!

Human memory is a mixture of fading remembered details. They're rather tenuously connected, disorganized and *vulnerable to corruption*, especially by new information. The new information *replaces* the old information. And Mind LTD isn't even *aware* that the old information is being *corrupted* by the new stuff!

You think anyone will notice that this memory *isn't the same* as the last time we remixed it?

You mean we've remixed it *before*?

I don't remember *that*.

"The only states of consciousness
that we naturally deal with
are found in personal consciousnesses,
minds, selves, concrete particular I's and you's.
Each of these minds
keeps its own thought to itself.
There is no giving or bartering
between them."

   -- *William James*, The Principles of Psychology

3

• • •

PRIMING CONSCIOUSNESS

Here's a most basic experiment to keep in mind as you read through this chapter and the succeeding ones.

You are sitting in front of a screen that flashes words for just an instant, and the experimenter, as have zillions of psychologists before her, is checking to see how long it takes you to recognize the word.

You are shown words such as "Yule," "catamaran," "divine." All take roughly the same time to register in consciousness.

Now you are shown "apple" and the same thing happens. But if you are shown "pear" just after you see "apple," you register it faster than if you had seen "pear" after "catamaran."

This is a simple experiment, and it can be repeated using sounds and other media.

And it's not just word associations; recent events change our minds much more than we'd believe. If you find money unexpectedly, your opinions on a whole host of issues (how happy you are in life, prospects for war) change markedly. Some translate almost metaphorically: if you get a cold cup of coffee vs. a hot one, you are likely to judge a person as, well, "colder" than before, and the same is true with a hottie. Our view of the world shifts substantially from moment to moment depending on where we've just been.

PRIME TIME

The mind becomes primed from one moment to the next, depending on environment or subject categories.

Sometimes this manipulation is deliberate, as it is with romancing or with real estate: realtors "stage" homes, making them feel warm and inviting which may cost several thousand to do so, but it reaps increased sales prices in the scores of thousands. Most often, we are at the mercy of events, and we are unconscious of our own "attitude meter" swinging back and forth, our consciousness adrift.

I submit that these are some of psychology's most important and unrecognized demonstrations.

• • •

Why should it be necessary for the mind to be so simple? And how does the mind, so simple, adapt to such different circumstances? A call from our aunt means that we have to remember the last time Uncle Tim went into the hospital for, what was it, diabetes? We might have to try to use our French and meat knowledge to speak to the butcher. A friend mentions the 49ers, and we have to know football rules, what happened over the past seasons, whether you went to a game with him or watched one on TV. If you think of all the people you know and all the TV programs you follow, all the news stories you read and all the sports teams, you will see that at any moment you may wish to access one of a million points of information. And you never know what's coming up in life.

The same thing happens when we move around, too. When you drive a long distance, you rarely remember the streets at your destination, but when you get there, you recall "Aunt Jennie's place is the second left after the Krispy Kreme sign,

I think," but you may not have been able to access that info from far away. Local cues (the blue beer sign, the water tower) nudge your memory into a new configuration. The locale becomes local.

This adaptability is the centerpiece of humanity. It enables our kind to live high in the Andes, in the scorching and barren Kalahari, or even in central Tokyo. And, perhaps more importantly for our past, it enabled us to migrate from place to place, to follow the appearance of wild fruits and the migrations of game. And to remember where to go and where to find things once we got there. It's obvious when you travel back home, or to a hotel where you've stayed before. All of a sudden you might remember to turn left to get coffee in the morning, something you couldn't remember and have not thought of, since you'd been there earlier.

Every day, every moment we are "primed," to use the technical term, to think in one way or another. Most of this priming allows us to navigate complex situations with little information in "mind" -- another example of how changeable and limited is mental life.

There's a lot to know in life, but we don't want to (can't really) know it, see it, think of it or remember it all at once. We can't keep it all "in mind."

As we grow from infancy to adulthood, our "idea" of "what's goin' on" in the world elaborates. And there's a lot to know: how a ball will fall, what a raised eyebrow from your mother means, which way a leaf will blow in the wind, what a cat wants when it mews, when to eat the sweets at dinner, when to expect happy endings in the movies, what those funny marks mean when you try to read, what an investor does, how to cook broccoli, and the millions of other routines we usually know. We, early on, develop expectations; a child takes a quantum leap in her knowledge of the world when she realizes that an object she has seen placed behind a screen is still there, even though hidden from view. Before that, she had no idea of a world existing unseen. This idea is the way we come to *re*-present our little world when we blink our eyes, so that it continues without our noticing the interruption.

•   •   •

In Susan Engel's book *Context is Everything*, the author describes a time when she and her sister baked a cake for her mother's birthday party. She could almost smell it and taste the icing and the creamy yellow cake and the look of delight in her mother's eyes. She discussed the party once with her sister, and her sister said: "You've got it all wrong, you weren't even there, you were in college at the time." Jane had "*re*-membered" the event based only on shared discussions.

We don't remember by "viewing" a kind of "slide" stored somewhere, as we might a slideshow of that cabin at the lake we rented a few years ago. Rather, we compute our memories and, really, our lives anew each time, online, with whatever information we have around.

That means, for instance, that psychologist Elizabeth Loftus' work on introducing information after an event works this way: the later information is just incorporated into the memory which then seems as real as an untampered one. Loftus' work involves showing a scene, such as cars moving, and later asking people something like "How fast were they moving?" or "How fast were they moving when the cars crashed into each other?" While no crash was shown, those who heard the latter question remembered -- that is reconstructed -- a crash more often than did those who were only asked about the speed of the cars. Schoolchildren are easily manipulated this way, even into "believing" they saw sexual molestation when none occurred, just by the asking of questions like "Did you see Mr. Hamilton touching Sarah?" or, even better, "What happened after Mr. Hamilton touched Sarah; did she cry?" There's a "demand" made by such questions, and we, believers in the rightness of others, often come to accept them. And the younger we are, the easier this new representation of what happened gets inside our heads.

This is how "recovered" memories, memories that are influenced by alter suggestions, get formed. They're not "*re*-covered," but "*re*-computed" in the same way all our memories are created. Sometimes there's malice in those who try to frame a memory, sometimes it happens by accident. Either way, the result can be tragic. Following is one such example.

I WAS CERTAIN BUT I WAS WRONG
by Jennifer Thompson
from *The New York Times* editorial page

In 1984 I was a 22-year-old college student with a grade point average of 4.0, and I really wanted to do something with my life. One night someone broke into my apartment, put a knife to my throat and raped me.

During my ordeal, some of my determination took an urgent new direction. I studied every single detail on the rapist's face. I looked at his hairline; I looked for scars, for tattoos, for anything that would help me identify him. When and if I survived the attack, I was going to make sure that he was put in prison and he was going to rot.

When I went to the police department later that day, I worked on a composite sketch to the very best of my ability. I looked through hundreds of noses and eyes and eyebrows and hairlines and nostrils and lips. Several days later, looking at a series of police photos, I identified my attacker. I knew this was the man. I was completely confident. I was sure.

I picked the same man in a lineup. Again, I was sure. I knew it. I had picked the right guy, and he was going to go to jail. If there was the possibility of a death sentence, I wanted him to die. I wanted to flip the switch.

When the case went to trial in 1986, I stood up on the stand, put my hand on the Bible and swore to tell the truth. Based on my testimony, Ronald Junior Cotton was sentenced to prison for life. It was the happiest day of my life because I could begin to put it all behind me.

In 1987, the case was retried because an appellate court had overturned Ronald Cotton's conviction. During a pretrial hearing, I learned that another man had supposedly claimed to be my attacker and was bragging about it in the same prison wing where Ronald Cotton was being held. This man, Bobby Poole, was brought into court, and I was asked, "Ms. Thompson, have you ever seen this man?"

I answered: "I have never seen him in my life. I have no idea who he is."

Ronald Cotton was sentenced again to two life sentences. Ronald Cotton was never going to see light; he was never going to get out; he was never going to hurt another woman; he was never going to rape another woman.

In 1995, 11 years after I had first identified Ronald Cotton, I was asked to provide a blood sample so that DNA tests could be run on evidence from the rape. I agreed because I knew that Ronald Cotton had raped me and DNA was only going to confirm that. The test would allow me to move on once and for all.

I will never forget the day I learned about the DNA results. I was standing in my kitchen when the detective and the district attorney visited. They were good and decent people who were trying to do their jobs -- as I had done mine, as anyone would try to do the right thing. They told me: "Ronald Cotton didn't rape you. It was Bobby Poole."

The man I was so sure I had never seen in my life was the man who was inches from my throat, who raped me, who hurt me, who took my spirit away, who robbed me of my soul. And the man I had identified so emphatically on so many occasions was absolutely innocent.

Ronald Cotton was released from prison after serving 11 years. Bobby Poole pleaded guilty to raping me.

Ronald Cotton and I are the same age, so I knew what he had missed during those 11 years. My life had gone on. I had gotten married. I had graduated from college. I worked. I was a parent. Ronald Cotton hadn't gotten to do any of that.

Mr. Cotton and I have now crossed the boundaries of both the terrible way we came together and our racial difference (he is black and I am white) and have become friends. Although he is now moving on with his own life, I live with constant anguish that my profound mistake cost him so dearly. I cannot begin to imagine what would have happened had my mistaken identification occurred in a capital case.

And the mistakes can be much more subtle as well, so much so that we'd never be aware of them. In a study by Patricia Devine, students saw a list of words flashed very, very quickly, so as to be unrecognizable:

basketball

jazz

ghetto

slavery

emancipation

harlem

You might note that these connect with the stereotype of a black American. No one could recognize the words, but when afterwards they read vague reports about a man (not even identified as black!), they rated him as more hostile (which wasn't one of the words shown) than others who had seen neutral words.

There are many other studies like this, but the point is the same: countless times every day, we change our minds mindlessly as each new bit of information comes in. Because we're so flexible, we adapt -- often without knowing it and without knowing why. We change to suit circumstances, memories recreate themselves based on what just happened, and our attitudes shift based on what we're discussing (pollsters certainly know this, as do advertisers).

We certainly can't get rid of everything that happens to us and become less adaptable, but overcoming the unconscious biases requires that we know that the mind is so unstable.

We all know people who seem to have a good memory for faces but not for numbers. Other people can remember stories well but not directions. "Absent-minded professors" may remember specific details of the Peloponnesian War, but not where to go to pick up their laundry.

When we go out, I always remember what people had for dinner, and my wife remembers who was there. Some geniuses can pick out a late Bach sonata from just a few notes, yet when they leave the concert, they can't remember where they left their car keys.

There's certainly some information in memory, but memory gets created anew each time we need it; otherwise we'd be carrying around too much, like Funes the Memorious in Borge's *Ficciones*. He, you may recall, could remember everything, but he had so much "in mind" all the time that he couldn't *do* anything. Too much reality.

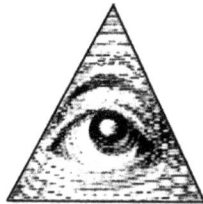

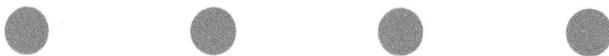

THE
MindReal
TOUR

••••

THE FOUNDATION
of MindReal

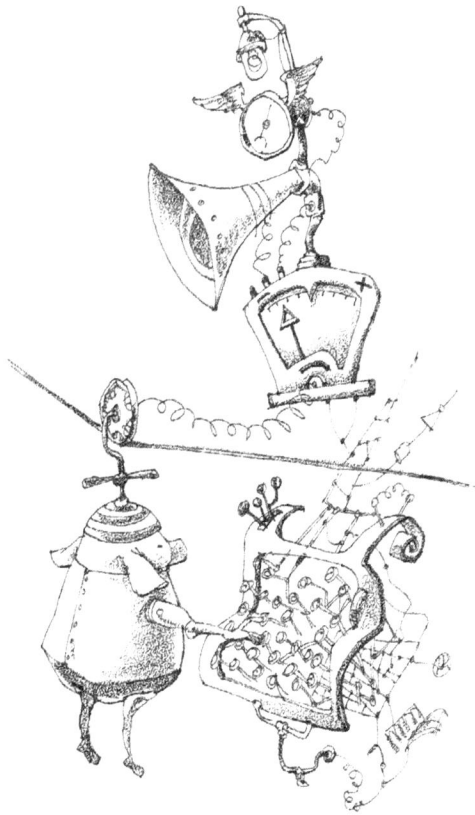

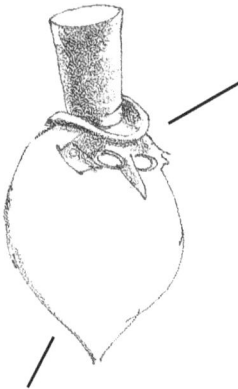

As well as selecting out their own tiny bits of reality, all creatures *make up* their *own MindReal*. The world appears totally different to *every organism*. A *fly* sees a whole *different* world than a *frog*, or a *dog*, and thus is alert to totally different opportunities and dangers.

The world according to any species other than your own would be very *strange indeed*, almost *unrecognizable*.

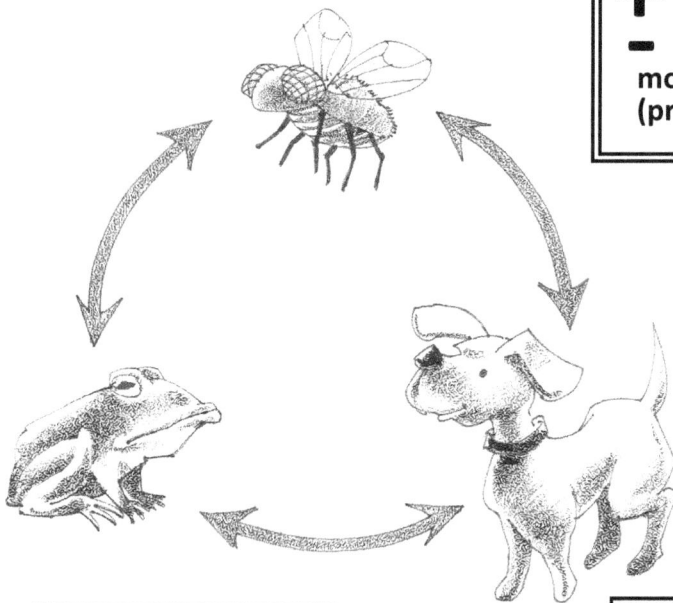

+ seek dogshit

− avoid quick-moving things (predators)

+ seek moving black dots (flies)

− avoid large looming shapes (predators)

+ seek small chunks of meat

− avoid rival dogshit

But the devices used to create various *MindReals* across the animal kingdom are similar. For instance, this little device here is found in most organisms. I call it **the comparometer**. It **compares** new information with old. Evolution *favors* this simple **comparison** process over the far more difficult process of measuring things *absolutely*. No matter how *strong* or *weak* the input signal, the comparometer will read zero unless there is some **change** in the input. In other words, this is the machine that explains the expression, *"you'll get used to it."*

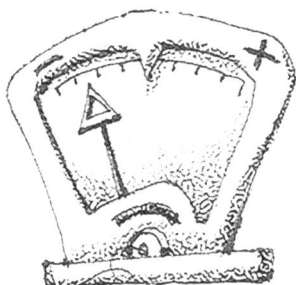

THE COMPAROMETER

Why would that be *advantageous*? I'd have thought it would be better to be able to know what was really going on rather than how things **compared** from one moment to the next.

It's a matter of survival! Here lemme demonstrate by assuming the form of a frog....

The *most important* information for living things is to know whether they need to take action in response to any *changes* in their *environment.*

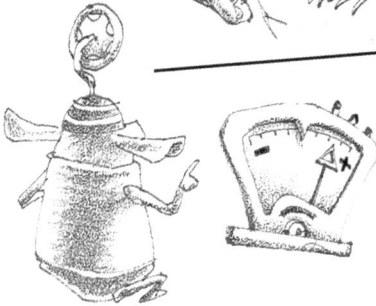

Light decreasing... *quicker* and *quicker,* looks like trouble...*oi, get outta there!*

Usually in a *very short period* of time.

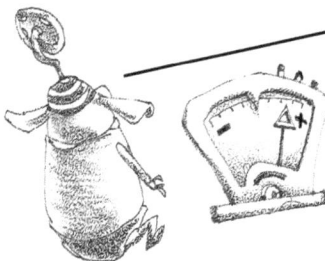

Whew! Got outta there *just in time.* What would I do *without* this *comparometer!*

WITH COMPAROMETER

However, if my mind spends *too much time* measuring the absolute intensity of the signals from *Reality* it would take *so long* that...

Light intensity reading now at 67%, 66%, 65%, 64%, 63%, 62%, 61%, 60%, 59%, 58%, 57%, 56%, 55%, 54%, 53%, 52%, 51%, 50%, 49%, 48%, 47%, 46%, 45%, 44%, 43%, 42%, 41%, 40%, 39%, 38%, 37%, 36%, 35%, 34%, 33%, 32%, 31%, 30%, 29%, 28%, 27%, 26%, 25%, 24%, 23%, 22%, 21%, 20%...

CHOMP!

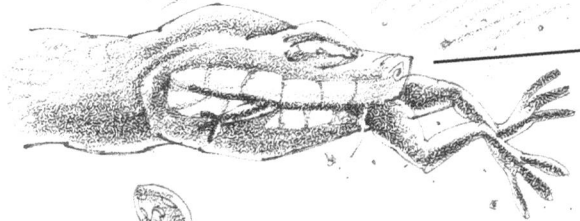

....*mmmf gmphlg bfgh*....

...18%, 15%, 10%, 0%...*oops*, I think we're *finished*...

WITHOUT COMPAROMETER

It seemed like such a good way of doing business. After all, efficiency means survival. I found I could just leave Mind LTD workers to get on with the job while I got on with mine.

Say, boss, this thing works *great* detecting *change* in temperature and light and so on...how about we use it for just about everything else we do, too?

Yeah, *yeah*, whatever... so long as it *works*...

But here's where you run into trouble: so long as the *comparometer* reads *zero*, and Mind LTD doesn't detect change, you can be shifted into perverse thinking that might *surprise* you. Here are some of the things you are capable of thinking so long as *everyone else* is *also* doing it. You measure the propriety of your own behavior *compared to* the behavior of those *around you*.

Guess it's *OK* to leave that woman *bleeding* on the sidewalk.

Guess it's *OK* to deliver a *450-volt electric shock* to the guy strapped in that chair.

Guess it's *OK* to wear these *ridiculous ugly-colored bell-bottoms*, even though my bum looks big in them and my stomach *hangs* over the belt.

Guess it's *OK* to keep watching TV, even though I can hear *screaming* outside.

Guess it's *OK* to *torture* this helpless person, just because somebody *told* me to.

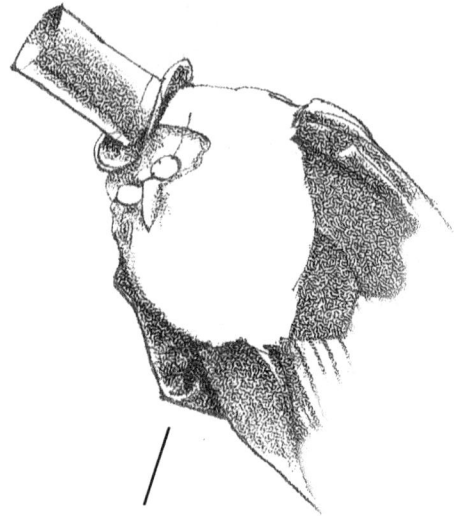

Mind LTD just doesn't have *time* to *contemplate* things that do not change. Since danger and opportunity are *both* linked with change, Mind LTD is *stirred into action* by the quick change and the *most recent* information.

IN EMERGENCY

BREAK GLASS

NEAUGHH!

What was *that*?

If a small portion of *Reality* suggests a *new change* in circumstances, you can bet this will get *most* of the attention of Mind LTD!

CONSCIOUSNESS

SUBCONSCIOUS
AWARENESS

PRECONSCIOUSNESS

UNCONSCIOUSNESS

CONSCIOUS &
UNCONSCIOUS
PROCESSING

UNCONSCIOUS
MOTIVATION

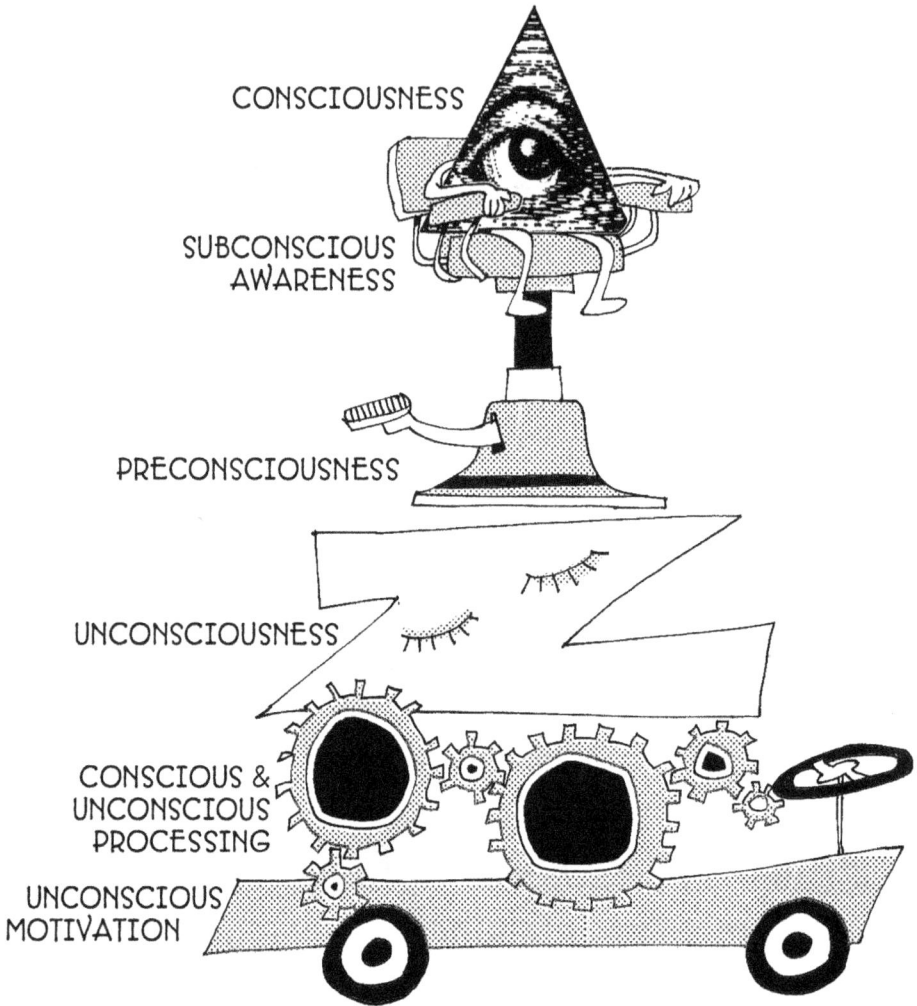

You can describe this jumble of antiquated survival *policies, unseen urges, automatic mind work,* and *prejudices* by any set of terms you like, but in the end, to do so is akin to describing a *ramshackle house* as a *great work of architecture.*

Sure, it's been *useful* for humans to imagine there's a *sensible structure* behind their minds, but it only serves to give rise to *mistaken ideas* about *me* and my job.

(sigh) And to think, all those years of psychotherapy were just patching up a *mess* from top to bottom...

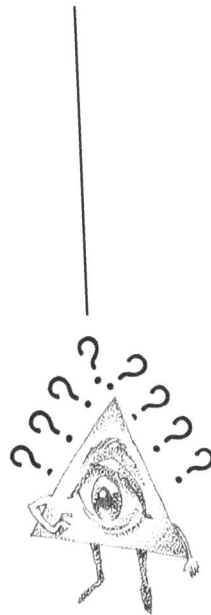

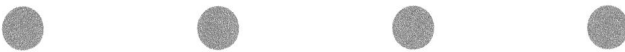

We see that the mind is at every stage a theatre of simultaneous possibilities. Consciousness consists in the comparison of these with each other, the selection of some, and the suppression of others, of the rest by the reinforcing and inhibiting agency of attention. The highest and most celebrated mental products are filtered from the data chosen by the faculty below that, which mass was in turn sifted from a still larger amount of simpler material, and so on. The mind, in short, works on this block of stone. In a sense, the statue stood there from eternity. But there were a thousand different ones beside it. The sculptor alone is to thank for having extracted this one from the rest. ...Other minds, other worlds, from the same monotonous and inexpressive chaos! My world is but one in a million, alike embedded and alike real to those who may abstract them. How different must be the world in the consciousness of ants, cuttle-fish, or crab!

-- *William James*

4

● ● ● ●

MIXING AND REMIXING THE
ELEMENTS OF EXPERIENCE

Consider the life of the mind from an engineering, rather than our internal, standpoint, and one fact leaps out: what registers inside of the mind is much less than what's really going on in the world. That's obvious, for how could you be cognizant of everything at once? But a bit less obvious is the fact that, even when restricting our attention to just a small portion of what's before us -- say, a person walking through a large field -- the contents of the mind's shell are way less than a trillionth of what's outside. Tekkies call "bandwidth" the amount of information that it is possible to process at any moment. Playing a video, for example, processes far more than playing an MP3 audio file

The world outside is silent, dull. It could be called odorless, colorless and tasteless, for there is no color in nature, no sound, no touch, no smell. All these wonders exist inside the shell that the mind creates for us to live in. Out of the few, forlorn signals that get inside, we create an entire world, in the same way as do architects who create whole buildings using only lines on paper. Consider an average telephone call in which you immediately recognize a friend's voice. First, and most obviously, there's no long tube carrying her or his actual vocals; instead, a microphone transmits them electronically, just as a stereo transmits music. And the telephone is different in another way: the information

MIND FILTERING

A FEW DOZEN BITS PER SECOND LEAK THROUGH

INFORMATION DELUGE (BITS PER SEC)

BANDWIDTH JAM
Our mind blocks most of the signals from reality and lets in only a tiny trickle of information.

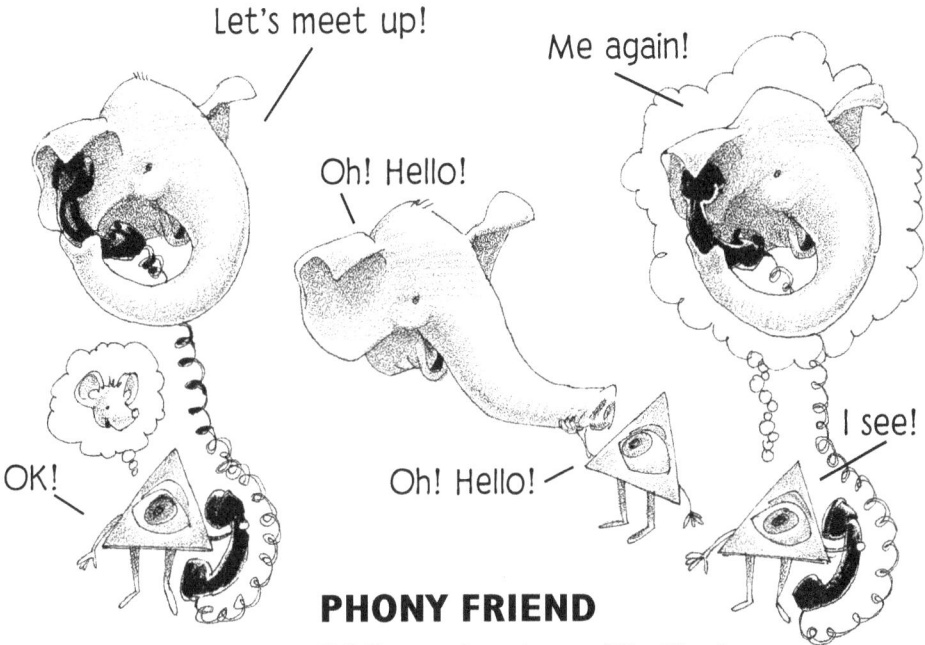

PHONY FRIEND

While on the phone, MindReal recreates a far more fleshed-out version of a friend compared to someone we haven't yet met in person.

transmitted is far less than 5% of the sounds that the person speaks. It is we, on the receiving end, who fill in the rest. You can note this the next time you "meet" a person only on the phone. You will produce an estimate of the voice. And once you've met, the next phone call will sound like the person because you now have the blueprint of the person's voice.

The important point is that, compared with what's really out there, what we experience of it is so tiny as to be almost lost. Each animal's selection is different, as it blinds its owner to most of the world in order to avoid dangers and exploit opportunities.

But the little amount that we perceive is precious, for it is how we manipulate and get through our entire lives. Let's look at the bandwidth of information in the external world and in ours.

When somebody (in the soon-to-be-old days) draws a cartoon, they have to draw it to be shown at 24 frames per second. If Tweety Bird is moving through the sky, you may notice that the sky doesn't move much from moment to moment, but the bird does. To simplify the work, cartoonists draw only those parts of the frame that are changed from the previous ones.

And this is how we simplify the world, as well. When something is constant (think about your weight against the chair; did

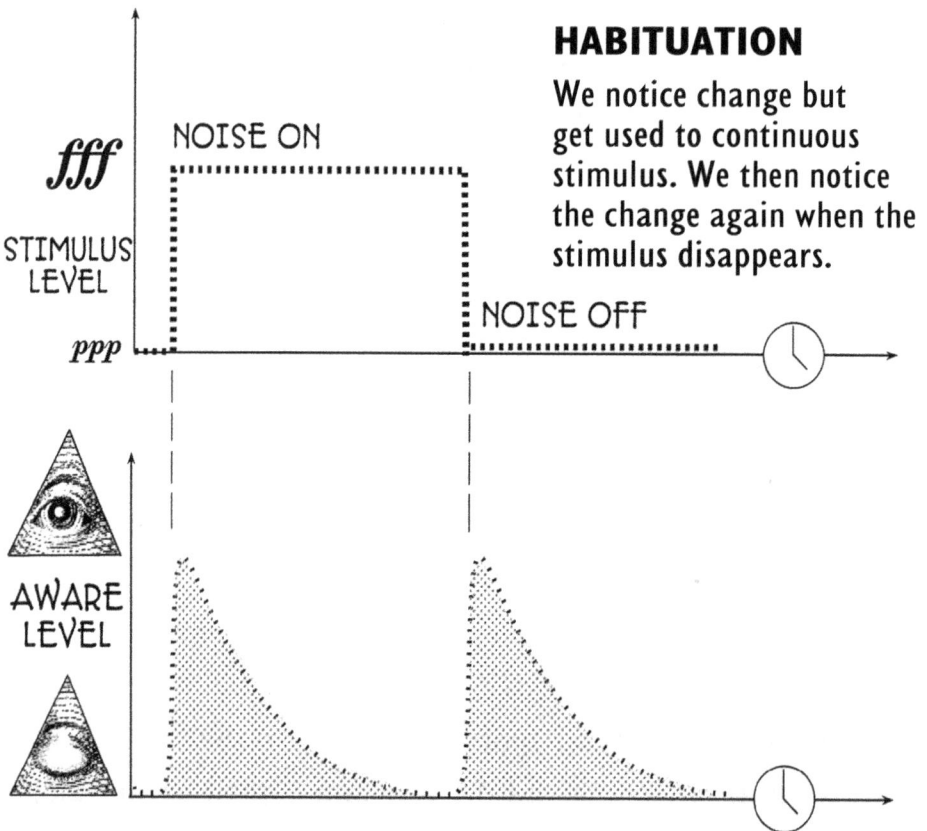

HABITUATION

We notice change but get used to continuous stimulus. We then notice the change again when the stimulus disappears.

you notice it?), we tune it out, and we focus and respond only to changes. Technically this is called "habituation"; a neuron will gradually decrease responding to the same stimulus. This has wide applications, but, for us, the first is that what moves gets noted, and what stays still goes away. The mind is tuned to "The News."

Although there is an astronomical amount of information in the world, human experience is limited to the visual, audible, olfactory, taste and tactile channels. In addition to telling us about

SIGHT

HEARING

SMELL

SENSES

Information from Reality is filtered out by these external and internal senses.

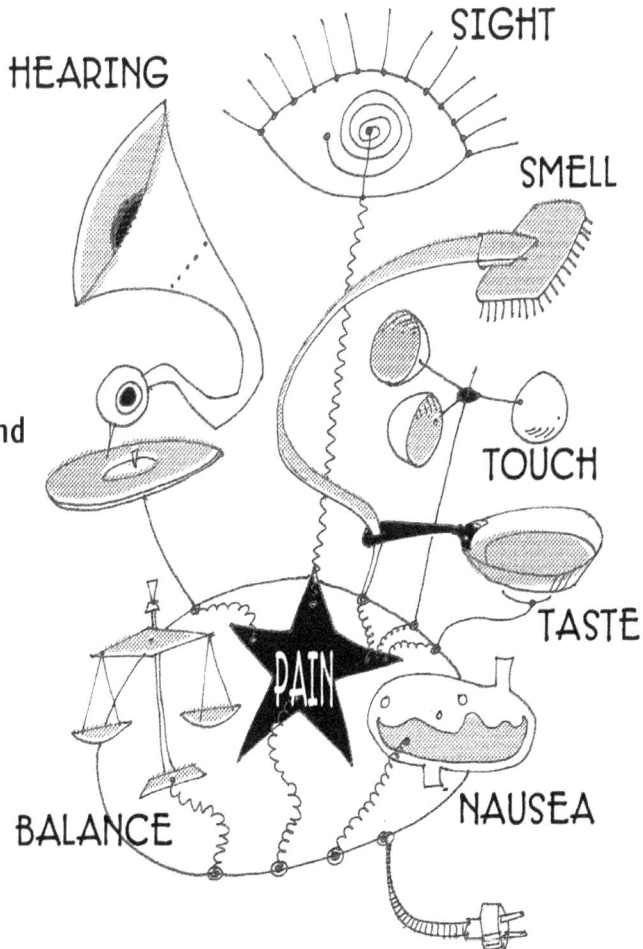

TOUCH

TASTE

PAIN

BALANCE

NAUSEA

the world "out there," our senses inform us about the world of our bodies, helping us maintain balance, coordinate and control our movements, and sense internal conditions such as pain and nausea. Most of our experience of the world is of change: the sun coming up, a sudden loud noise, a change in the weather.

Our sensory systems operate to notice the beginnings and endings of events. When an air conditioner turns on in a room, you notice the hum. Soon you become habituated, or accustomed, to the noise. When it turns off, you again take note, this time because of the sudden *absence* of the noise. The senses are thus interested in news; loosely speaking, their operation follows the axiom, "Call me when something new happens."

• •

From PSYCHOLOGY: THE STUDY OF HUMAN EXPERIENCE

Consider an animal that simplifies even more than we do. Jerome Lettvin and his associates at Massachusetts Institute of Technology devised an experiment in which visual stimulation was offered to one eye of an immobilized frog. The frog was placed so that its eye was at the center of a hemisphere seven inches in radius. Small objects were placed in different positions on the inner surface of this hemisphere by means of magnets and could be moved around in the space inside the hemisphere. The investigators measured "what the frog's eye tells the frog's brain" -- that is, the electrical impulses sent to the brain by the eye. However, when an assortment of objects, colors, and patterns were shown to the frog, the investigators noticed a remarkable phenomenon. Despite the great variety of stimuli presented, the eye sent only four kinds of "messages" to the brain. These four

The first need for any animal is to find out what is happening in the world and how to respond to it. The world is full of events, from simple wind shifts, sunrises and miniscule movement of particles in the air, to the sudden alighting of hawks. The earth shifts its large surface plates, rotates upon its axis and moves around the sun. On its surface are millions of tiny particles and vast populations of bacteria. Pressure waves (sounds) and radiant electromagnetic energy fill the air.

When you make a telephone call, you don't want to hear all possible human voices. Similarly, the mind needs to limit the information it receives to a small fraction of that actually present in the outside world. It extracts from the cacophony of the entire

● ●

messages contained information relating directly to the two most important aspects of a frog's survival: obtaining food and escaping danger. The first message provided a general outline of the environment. Two of the messages formed a kind of bug-perceiving system: one detected moving edges and the other responded to small, dark objects entering the field of vision. Frogs catch and eat only live insects. A frog surrounded by food that did not move would starve to death because it has no means for detecting unmoving objects. The fourth message responded to sudden decreases in light, as would happen if a large enemy approached. The frog's brain is "wired" to ignore all but a very few specific types of information. Although higher-level animals, ourselves included, are not as restricted in sensory experience as the frog, the sensory systems of all animals simplify their organism's world by the act of selection.

··· | | | ···

"big world" a specialized "small world" in which an individual organism can act and live. We have only the operations of sight, hearing, taste, smell and touch available to us. But each sense receives only a limited range of stimuli. The eye, for instance, responds to only a minute portion (one-trillionth) of the entire spectrum of radiant electromagnetic energy.

Ordinary observation of the world seems to yield specific, different objects: cats and chocolate cakes, mountains and water. But think about it: How could a cat, or an image of a cat, get inside our brain? It doesn't enter directly; there are no "cat paths" inside us. And if there were such paths, what about buildings, trees, grass and sky? Obviously, we don't have a single brain area for perceiving each and everything in the world.

How, then, do we perceive such a huge variety of things? No one knows for sure, but there must first be a process of deconstruction of the physical world, so that selected parts of the information available enter the nervous system. Deconstruction means just what it sounds like, a breakup of a whole object into its parts. The technical task for psychologists and other analysts of sensation is to determine which components of the outside world our brain analyzes, and how it assembles them later on.

The senses are both sensors and censors. Obviously, our senses show us the outside world, but if we were bombarded with all the sensations in the world, our experience would be extremely chaotic. The air in the room you are in is filled with various forms of energy: an entire spectrum of light, sound, radio waves and more. Yet, you are aware of only a small portion of that energy.

The light that we see is actually just a small portion of the band of radiant electromagnetic energy.

The senses select what is important and keep the rest of the world out. And each sense has evolved to extract a very specific kind of information. You see light; you do not hear it. You cannot taste an apricot by squeezing it into your ear. Each organism's sensory system simplifies the world to detect only what it needs. The cat is a nocturnal animal and so needs its reflective eyes to see in the dark; insects see infrared radiation, which we feel as warmth; and a frog sees only things that move.

Again, when an event continues for a while, we stop notic-

PROFOUND EXPERIMENT

The same bowl of water feels different to different observers when compared to water at another temperature.

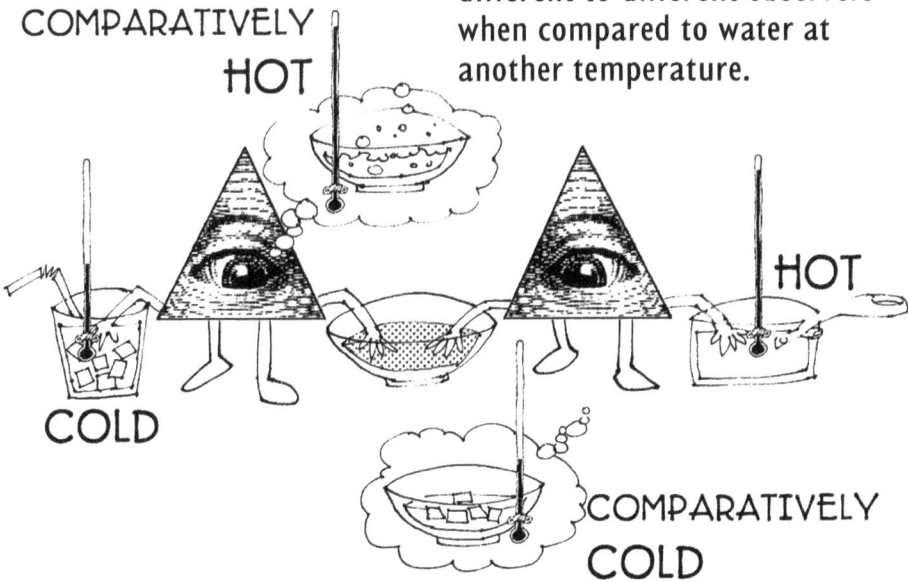

COMPARATIVELY HOT

COLD

HOT

COMPARATIVELY COLD

ing it. The air conditioner in the room, the noise of the street, our breathing -- all seem to disappear. This happens because our senses respond vigorously to beginnings and endings of events and less to constant stimulation. This sensory adaptation reduces the number of irrelevant sensations, allowing us to focus on new events in the environment.

Although each sensory system can discriminate millions of gradients of stimulation, it does not have a specific receptor for, say, each shade of color or each tone of sound. This is an important part of how we are built: since we rarely experience the exact situation twice, it would be uneconomical to have a system that responds in a different way to each new stimulus. Thus, sensory systems operate primarily by comparison. Judgments are comparative: the color seen at one moment is brighter or redder than the previous one; a sound is louder or more complex than an earlier one.

Here is a well-known demonstration of sensory adaptation, change and comparison. Fill three bowls with water: one hot, one cold and one tepid. Put one hand in the hot water and the other in the cold water. Wait a few moments. Now place both hands in the tepid bowl. Notice that the hand that was in the hot water feels cold, while the hand that was in the cold water feels warm. Both hands had adapted to their relative temperatures. Then, when the hands were put in the tepid bowl, they sensed a change. Although both hands were in the same bowl of water, each responded differently to it. The particular message of change that each hand signaled to the brain was based on a comparison of two events.

A sensory change is a difference in a stimulus from one moment to the next. One sensation always follows and precedes another, so one stimulus is louder, softer, brighter, dimmer, warmer, colder, greener or redder than something else. We compare relative differences between stimuli. Recall this demonstration: put a three-way bulb (50-100-150 watt) in a lamp in a dark room. Turn on the lamp; the difference between darkness and the 50-watt illumination seems to be significant. But the next two increases in light -- from 50 to 100 watts and from 100 to 150 watts -- do not seem to be as great. Although the change in the physical stimulus (a difference of 50 watts) is the same each time, you hardly notice the difference of the two higher wattages.

But even that is much too much for the limits of the mind to do. If you're looking at a scene, or touching something, or listening to a conversation, everything that stays the same is dropped from the information transmission. It's a simple way to update. So animators can draw only a few changes in movement in a frame, leaving the background the same and producing a new image -- quite useful in saving effort, if you're doing 24 frames per second.

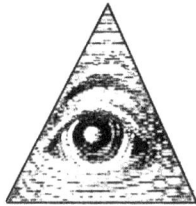

THE
MindReal
TOUR

• • • • •

WHEELING AND DEALING
WITH MindReal

So, do you *still* think
that you are in control?
Do you still think that
human behavior is directed
consciously?

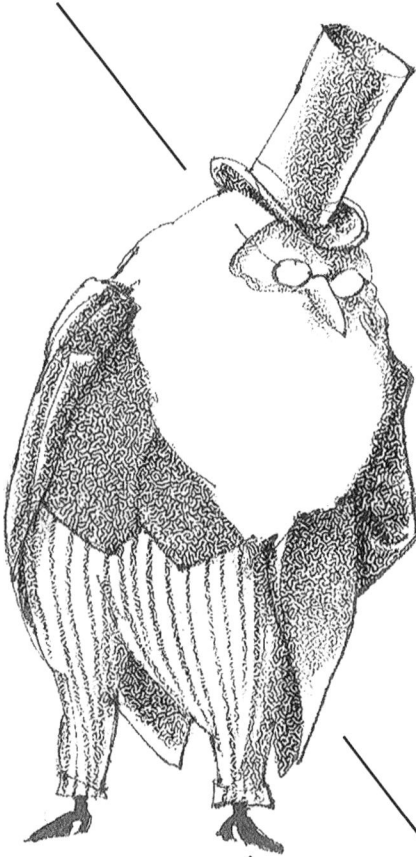

Somehow, I get the feeling
you're gonna tell me it's
not...

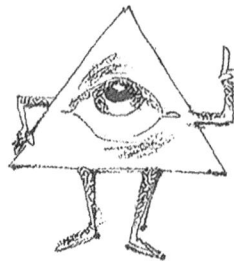

Precisely. Although you
feel as though you direct
behavior to a certain
extent, a great deal of
behavior is directed by
the environment--by what
happens around you.

Like I said before, this
accounts for the way
human behavior so often
confuses and *amazes*
you. You're so often
saying, "Why did I do that?
What was I *thinking*?"

That's because your mind wheels. Mind LTD is an **open-plan office** when it comes to dealing with most situations...different pig-headed minds are wheeled into place to handle different **situations.**

And sometimes, the **"wrong"** pig-head gets wheeled into place.

This accounts for why you are so **easily manipulated** by people who are **clever** enough to do your mind-wheeling for you.

What kind of a wizard could actually control my *Mind LTD*?

Well, there are plenty of *clever operators* out there who have an interest in *manipulating* your pig-heads. The *real pros* are those with something to *sell*.

HONEST WOODY'S USED CARS

*Ho boy, there's a real **schmuck** if I ever **saw one**. Looks like a real tire-kicker. Time to wheel in the ol' "Woody's Wheelin' Magic."*

A salesman?

Just watch this *wheeler dealer* operate on this customer. *Everything* he says is designed to wheel in just the right pig-heads. His *victim* will have no idea that his mind is being *messed around with.* He'll be made virtually *powerless* to resist (heh heh).

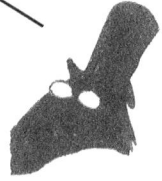

Howdy! You look like a pretty smart customer. How would you like to *save some money*?

Don't let this jerk mess with you. Don't forget what you came here for. Car dealers are all cunning operators. He's just trying to get me into a "YES" frame of mind.

Wheel in the "yes" pig-heads.

This baby just came in. You're the *first* person to see it! It's a *steal* at ten thousand! Want to take it for a *test drive*?

Ten thousand? You gotta be kidding! That's way too expensive!

That'll show this guy I'm no sucker. Who would pay that kind of money for this car?

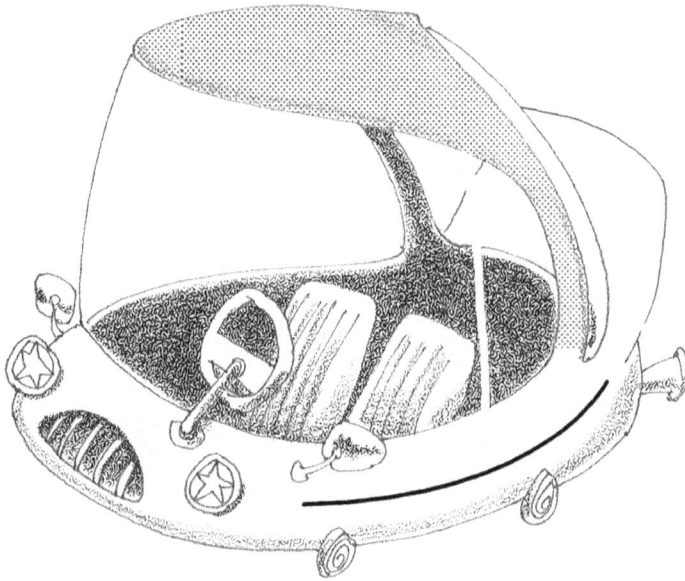

Wheel in
comparometer.

OK, I can see you **know** your cars. How about **this one**, then? It's only half the price of the first one.

Lemme tell ya a secret: the boss would **kill** me if she knew I told you that this car is really the **same** as the first one, only a **different marque**. It's a **steal**. I drive one myself!

Only half the price! How about that. That's pretty good. And it sounds like he's on my side, letting me in on a trade secret.

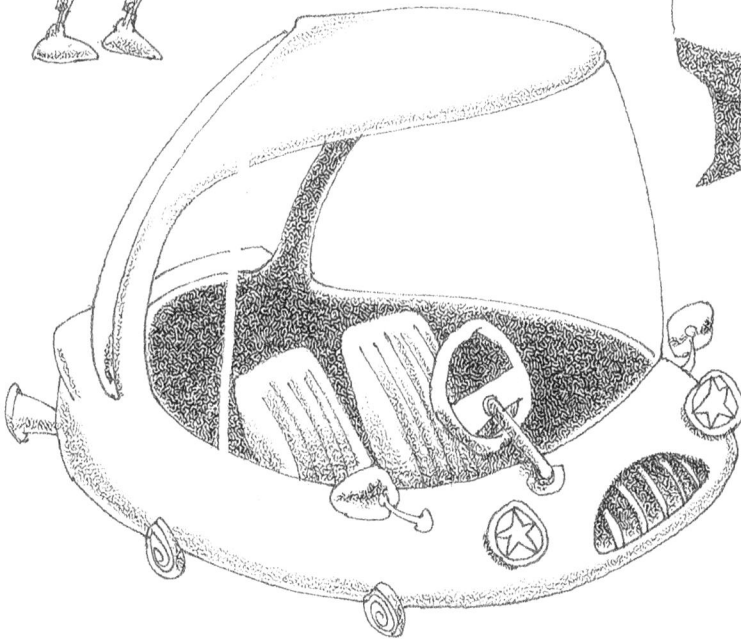

Wheel in **male-bonding, inspired-misogynist** *pig-heads.*

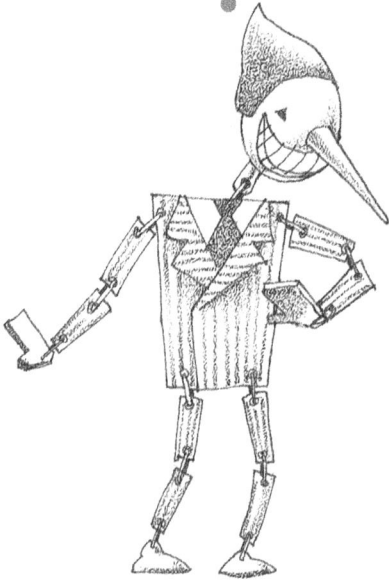

You're not worried about what the **wife** would say, are you? Who wears the trousers in **your** house? Don't you think you deserve something a bit **special**? You only live **once**. How does **0-60 in 4 seconds** sound to you, eh?

Gee, this is a **young man's car.** *Maybe I'd look* **younger and cooler** *in it and be more attractive to young women...the* **heck** *with the wife.*

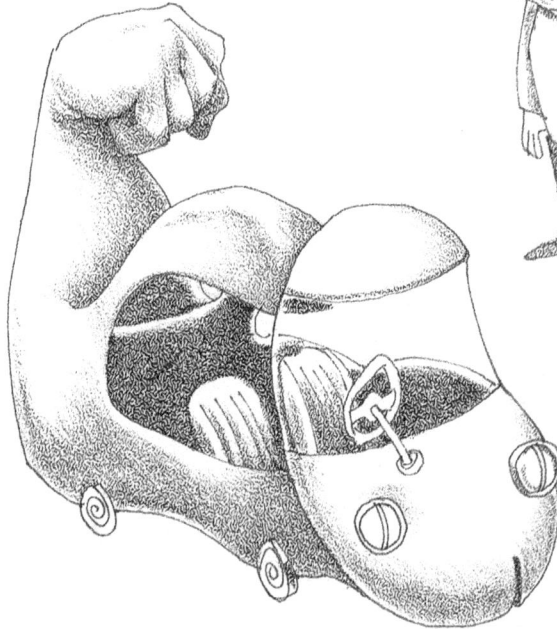

Wheel in **scarce- resource** *pig-heads.*

Why, *look*, here comes *another* customer to see the same car. Take as much time as you like. I'll tell him to *wait* while you look the car over. You had it *first*.

Aaarrrgh!! A **competitor** *wants this* **scarce resource***! Gotta* **grab** *it before my rival does!*

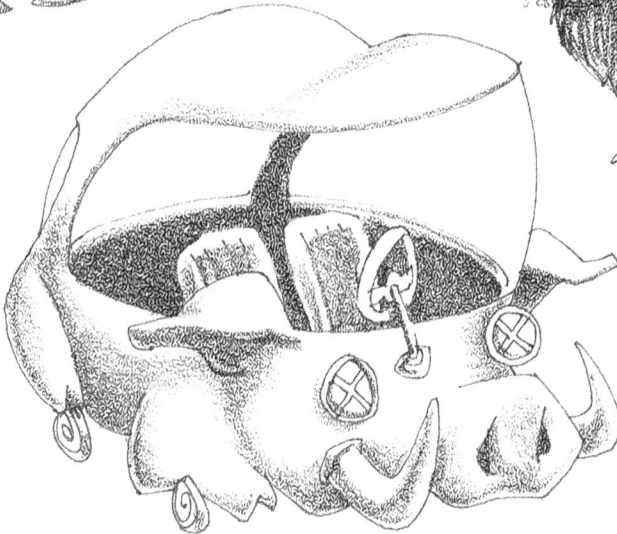

See ya
later pal!

$$$

Heh hey! I play 'em like
stringless puppets!

*Hey, what the **heck** is **that** all about?*

Don't ask ***me***. Buying a car
was the ***last*** thing on ***my***
mind. I thought we dropped
in to use the ***men's room...***

Wow, that song on the radio was playing when I **proposed!**

Multiple pig-heads can work at once. Here's an example of **piggy-backing** in action.

I gotta pee...

Once a driver, **never** a passenger again. I can't **relax** when he's driving...I keep putting the foot down on **imaginary brakes**.

Signal... left turn... check mirror... ease up on gas... tap brakes... step on gas... right nudge... etc., etc.

Oh *dear*. So the feeling of self-control is just *another part* of *MindReal*, and just as artificial.

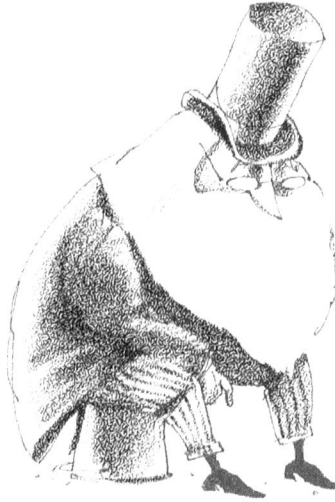

You're barely even behind the *wheel*, my friend.

Who's in control of this business, anyhow?

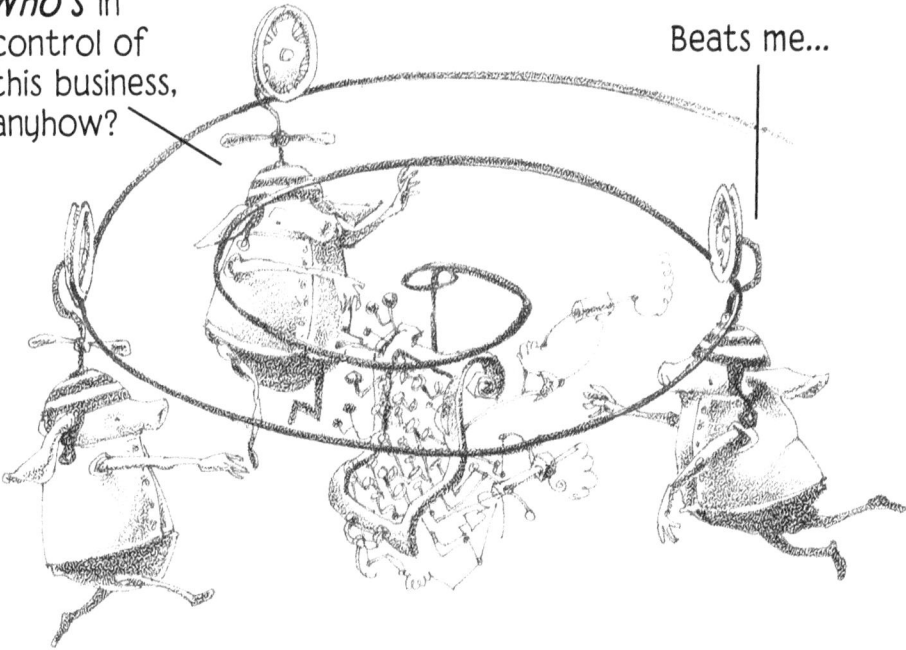

Beats me...

'O People!' shouted Nasrudin, running through the streets of his village, 'Know that I have lost my donkey. Anyone who brings it back will be given the donkey as a reward!'

'You must be mad,' said some spectators to this strange event.

'Not at all,' said Nasrudin, 'do you not know that the pleasure which you get when you find something that is lost is greater than the joy of possessing it?'

-- *Idries Shah*, Caravan of Dreams

5

• • • • •

THE MIND PLAYS
ITS LITTLE SHELL GAMES

The minds of all living beings have played their reality games for millions of years and developed their modes of action long before humanity sprang forth. Many of these procedures for judging the world are present in cows, frogs, and even in some insects.

The same mental routines which originally developed to judge brightness, taste, weight and suitability for eating now judge prices, politics and personalities. If you are carrying five pounds home on a walk and someone gives you their pack with 10 more pounds, it's suddenly very heavy. But if you're carrying 20 pounds home on a walk, and someone takes 5 pounds from your load, it suddenly feels light. The same process, the same comparison and adaptation, occurs when we buy things, when we evaluate government programs, and when we make dozens of routine decisions every day. Whether we consider something to be expensive or not is based almost entirely on what we've spent for it before. A reduction from $30 makes a price of $20 seem cheap; an increase from $10 makes a price of $20 seem expensive. It's the same process that we use to judge weight.

And the mind shifts, and the mind wheels, and the mind weaves everything together. Have you ever noticed that, after the resolution of their trauma, the grieving parents of a child who has been killed by a drunk driver often go on to form enduring

SAME OLD BRAIN

Human consciousness has had to adapt to a great variety of totally different environments.

HUMAN CONSCIOUSNESS HISTORICALLY
ABLE TO EMBRACE WIDE VARIETY
OF CONDITIONS AND ENVIRONMENTS

societies for the prevention of future drunk driving? They do so in part because the mind in place has been dramatically altered, shifted, by their experience. While preventing future drunk driving is a laudable aim, it was just as laudable before their child got killed, and afterwards it is too late to save their child.

Yet people who are at the head of these organizations are often ones who have suffered from a similar tragedy. It is simply because the mind is adaptive to the local situation in which it

* *

THE MIND SHIFTS
The mind shifts and wheels while consciousness remains unaware that it is not moving in a "straight line."

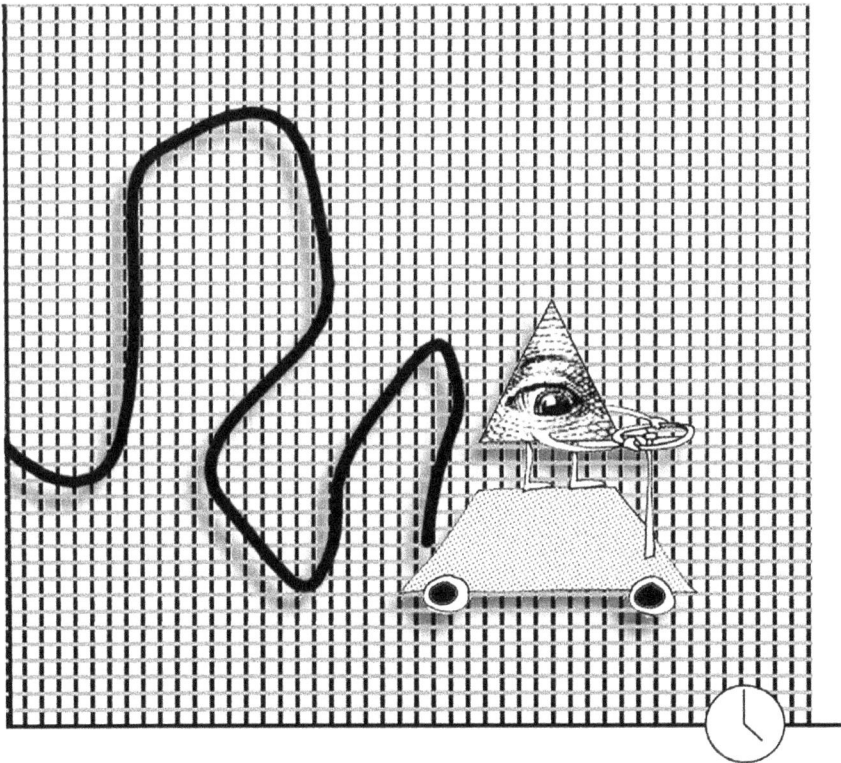

finds itself. If drunk driving becomes, as psychologists say, "salient," it means that opposing drunk driving will then become a more organized function of the person. It also means that we are dramatically prey to influences from sources that we might not like.

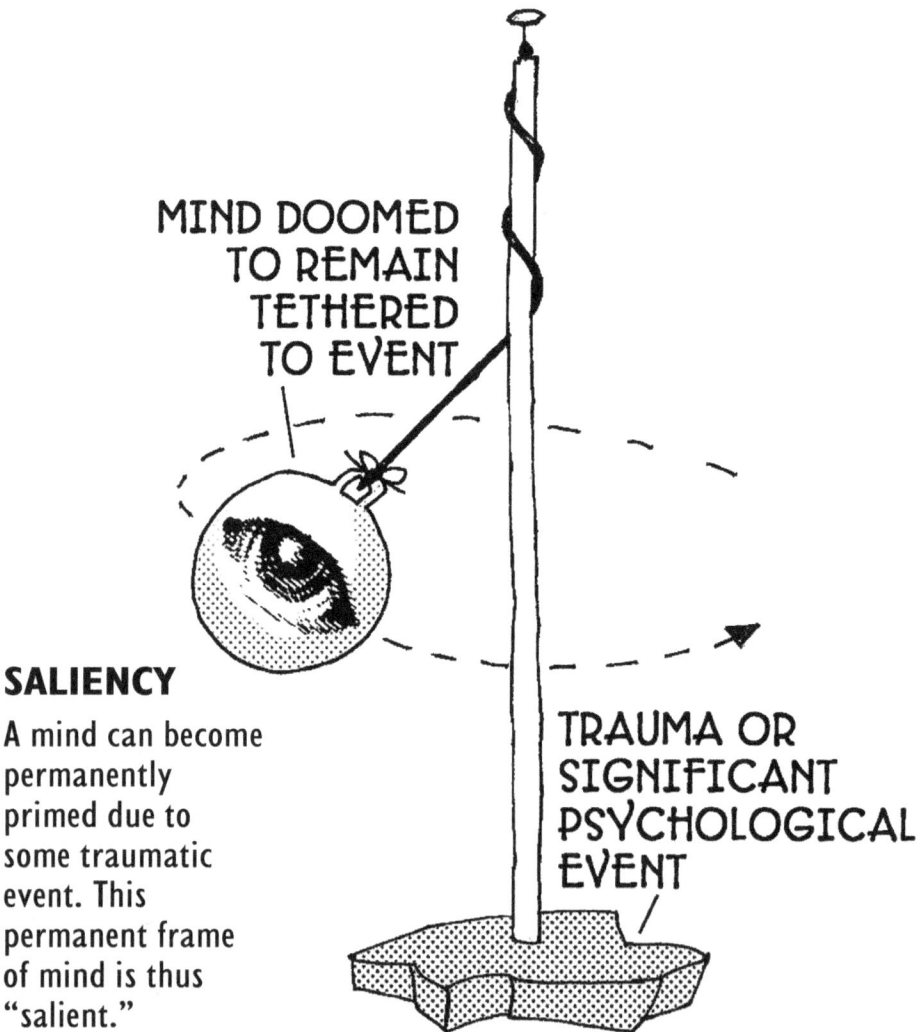

MIND DOOMED TO REMAIN TETHERED TO EVENT

SALIENCY

A mind can become permanently primed due to some traumatic event. This permanent frame of mind is thus "salient."

TRAUMA OR SIGNIFICANT PSYCHOLOGICAL EVENT

In effect, there are four basic policies of the mind:

1. *What have you done for me lately?*
We are extremely sensitive to recent information. Emotional upsets and bad feelings last awhile and then are forgiven. Terrible disasters like an air crash force our attention and that of the news media on airliners, for a moment, and all sorts of reforms are initiated, and then the spotlight goes away. A tennis star gets stabbed, and people say, "How can you let these tennis stars get so close to an unsupervised audience for so long? Any of them could have gotten killed." And two months later, you and I and just about everyone will have forgotten about protection for athletes. This week, though, it is high in our minds.

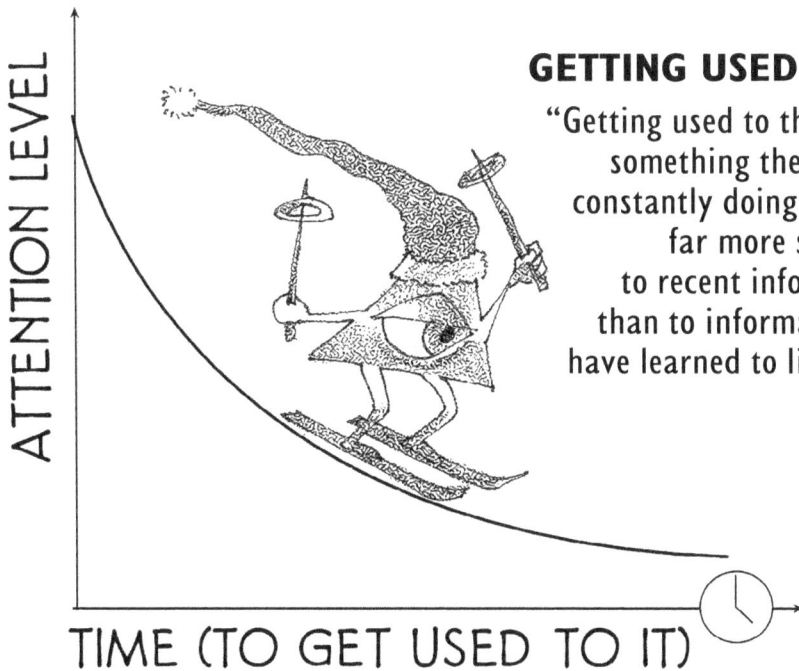

GETTING USED TO IT

"Getting used to things" is something the mind is constantly doing. We are far more sensitive to recent information than to information we have learned to live with.

ATTENTION LEVEL

TIME (TO GET USED TO IT)

2. *Don't call me unless anything new happens*
The mind is not specialized for the perception of reality; the mind is specialized for the perception of what you might call "the news." And if you look at the way the news media report the world, you will see that they do not, for instance, say, "The big news in Europe this evening is that 240 million people had a pleasant, quiet dinner at home." In fact, most evenings, that is the major story. Yet, when was the last time anybody said that on the news? In the same way, the mind is not organized to tell you what's actually going on, but rather is organized to

● ●

From MULTIMIND

A chemical spill in a Union Carbide plant in Bhopal, India, exposed hundreds of thousands of people to toxic fumes. It caused severe damage to the health of at least 20,000 people. Soon after the spill, stories appeared in the press describing the dangerous storage procedures in similar chemical plants in the United States. This event stimulated an investigation of such chemicals in the air in the United States and Western Europe that would have been done sooner were it not for the way human beings evolved to receive information. The slow release of toxins stays out of mind because the changes are slight. Then a disaster occurs, and all attention is fixed on it and similar problems. Magic Johnson revealed that he had AIDS. Funds for research were increased dramatically only a few days later. As an announcer on ABC News commented on an earlier, similar disclosure: "AIDS has received more attention in the few weeks after Rock Hudson's announcement than in the previous four years." AIDS, growing slowly and continuously, was suddenly noticed as a problem when a single famous person contracted it.

tell you what you need to act on next. Unexpected or extraordinary events have fast access to consciousness, while an unchanging background noise, or a constant weight or chronic problem, soon gets shunted into the background.

Thus, it is easy to raise money for emergencies such as for the few victims of a well-publicized disaster, or for Darfur relief, or for the protection of tennis athletes (although they probably don't need that much money). But it is much more difficult to raise money for the many victims of continuous malnutrition,

FATAL BUSINESS AS USUAL

We ignore everyday disasters such as deaths due to car accidents, but notice when a spectacular and unusual airplane accident occurs.

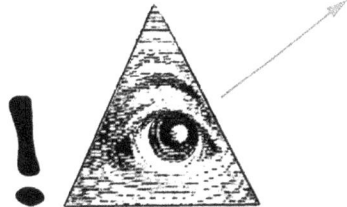

and for the effects of industrial groundwater pollution, and for worldwide starvation. We quickly respond to the sudden illumination of scarcity and danger, and to exciting events. Gradual changes in the world go unnoted, such as the massive global effects that are happening every day from overpopulation; while sharp changes, like a single airline disaster or some goofballs in Waco, Texas, blowing themselves up, make headlines. Far fewer people died in the Waco tragedy than died that same day on the roads of Europe, where they continue to be killed; but Waco gets our attention because it is a sharp change from the norm. We don't say, "another 75 people killed in road accidents in Europe this afternoon"; we don't say, "air pollution still high," although that is becoming part of our awareness.

3. *Comparison*
Comparison is a very important way we judge. "I am making more money than I did last year." "I am making less money." I once spoke to some Texans who were glum because their total net worth had dropped below $10 million, and $10 million was about the minimum needed to be a big player in the oil business.

THE COMPAROMETER

It is very difficult for us to judge anything absolutely, as we are wired to measure things only by comparison. We are most sensitive to the "deltas," or the different and changing aspects of things.

We use comparison because it simplifies judgment. Things are not heavy, but are heavier than we expect or were previously experiencing -- brighter, richer, more intelligent. We adapt to temperatures, to a level of income or net worth, to comfort, to taste; and we judge based on our assumed level of adaptation.

4. *Get to the point*
The mental system determines the meaning of any event and its relevance to the person. In the process, it throws out almost all information that reaches us. You probably saw 10 billion leaves last summer, but how many of them do you remember? A flash of red crossing your visual field may mean that your wife has driven home in her new red car, but you hardly notice what you really saw, instead you immediately think "she's home."

Most of us believe that the workings of the mind operate in a reasonable, stable, unchanging system. Reliable it is not. The mind is not stable; it wheels.

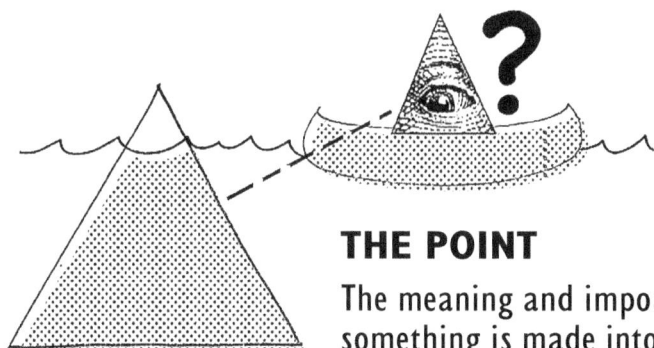

THE POINT
The meaning and importance of something is made into MindReal based on a relatively tiny chunk of information.

The mind is not neat; our mental apparatus is an amalgam of different circuits, of different priorities, of the evolutionary developments of different eras and, in fact, of different animals. The human mind was not constructed of new elements, but adapted whatever came before us. And what came before us were the orangutan, the bonobo, the lemur, the rat and the earthworm (among a few others).

The amalgamated nature of the mental system means that the human mind has separate routines lying aside one another. Each developed to serve a short-term purpose in millennia past. Evolution did not, unfortunately, work for the long term, but rather for the immediate exigencies of survival for individual animals. In biological evolution, there is a new deal every moment.

The mind didn't appear like a well-designed modern machine. It happened in a sloppy, slow, tedious manner, where circuits got added, where language simply got put atop a system that was already organized for handling life on earth -- which itself got piled atop a system that was quite well organized for handling life in the sea. That's why you need to adjust your internal mineral content so that it is about equal to that of a fish in the middle of the Mediterranean. That's why you need salt on a hot day, and why you need to worry so much about your intake of liquids.

This overall point is simple, I think, but the implication is not. The mind is nothing like what you've been taught to believe. There are many different access routes into it, and understanding its overall simplifications and policies can make you operate better and more effectively manage yourself and your own thought processes, as well as manage other people.

The mind is an inconsistent bundle of adaptations with different systems, some of which get called into play by accident, and some of which get called into play deliberately.

The major inroad into understanding the mind is becoming aware of the shifting nature of the underpinnings, like walking through waves on a sandy beach. If you've had enough self-observation to see the traps, you can begin to avoid them. A case in point: The normal strategies of the mind -- simplification and exclusion of information -- make us continuously overreact from the little information we get. When the news reports a murder in a distant city, we tend to think of the world as a murderous place. When someone famous comes down with breast cancer, it becomes a national concern. When you are frustrated in traffic, you can become frustrated about the progress of your business or the state of your marriage as well. Whatever enters consciousness is greatly over-emphasized.

Consider an experiment at a shopping center which brings much of this shifting, wheeling and dealing nature of the mind together. It took place a while ago, so the money levels are a bit off; but at the entrance to the shopping center, an experimenter placed a number of dollar bills. People coming into the shopping center and who picked up the dollar bill were followed and compared to others who entered at the same time.

Later, a number of opinions were requested at a polling booth, such as "How many times a week do you have sex?" "How happy are you with your refrigerator?" "How many repairs has your refrigerator had?" "What do you think the prospects are for nuclear war?" Those who found the dollar were having better sex lives, had refrigerators that they liked better and that had fewer repairs, and thought that nuclear war was less likely.

Leon Festinger found that when people approach a booth to place a bet on a horse, with the horse going out at 3 to 1, if you ask them what they think the odds are of the horse's winning, the average estimate is a little better than the posted odds. This

From EVOLUTION OF CONSCIOUSNESS

About 1977 . . . I was asked by the mayor of San Francisco to evaluate the fundraising techniques of a man who was then building up his Mission. He was very, very politically success-ful; he preached a message of racial harmony, and I went to a meeting to try to find out how he did it and whether these techniques would be suitable. How did he get twenty times as many volunteers as other people did with the same amount of effort?

Most of us just walk by all the time. I don't know about you, but I will admit that I do. This man, whose name was Jim, de-scribed one of his techniques: as you walk by, one of his people would say, "We have some printed letters addressed to people. And the envelopes are already stamped. All we want you to do is take five of these home. And lick the stamps, close the envelopes and just put them in the mail." Many people took it and when they passed the same street speaker later on, got recruited. A greater proportion, a very high proportion, twenty times the number of people who were given these envelopes to simply hold and mail, went back and helped this man's Mis-sion. I didn't like this guy. I have to say I was slightly envious, would be reasonable, because if you think the odds are really 2 to 1, you're quite happy to bet on a 3-to-1 shot. But after they place the bet, they think the odds *are even better than before*, because the mind in place has shifted, and people's estimates of what's going on, even their memories, are entirely fluid.

We are very easily misled.

I had a little bit of "why didn't I think of that," but I finally recommended that the city not use this guy, and his fundraising method. Then, in late 1977 and 1978, there were more stories about this man's Mission and how he got people in through all these really easily appealing procedures. Another way he would ask people to get in was by saying simply "just give us 10 cents." Now everybody has 10 cents. Even then, even in 1977, it was not a lot of money. So, you give someone a dime. What happens is that your mind wheels, like the drunk driver parents, the next time you are already a donor to this charity. The mind that is the donor isn't connected to the mind that has given 10 cents. So since you are a donor, you do more work. It's great stuff, if you are in business. It wasn't so great for this guy. Moreover, trouble ensued. And finally, this man, whose name was Jim Jones, took his group to Guyana in South America, where all these people thus recruited participated in Jonestown, which as you probably remember, until the latest thing from what we call Waco, Texas, has occurred, was one of the greatest American cult tragedies. Everyone was asking, "How did these people get recruited? How did it happen?" But it is very easy, it is very simple; you just have to know how.

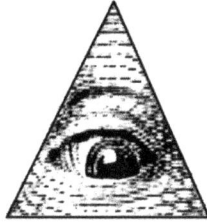

THE
MindReal
TOUR

• • • • • •

COPING WITH
MindReal

And now, let me show you just how much *trouble* Mind LTD has caused you *and* me.

The world took me
billions of years to
create, and yet your
blinkered ways have
pushed it all to the brink
of disaster.

W-what did I do
wrong?

That's the problem; you've done *nothing* wrong.

If it's *anyone's* fault, it's *mine*, and it's making me feel like hell. It's high time I just *retired*...

Why can't you just turn things around? After all, you're the *Almighty One*, aren't you?

That's what *you* think...as it turns out, I'm not so "Almighty" afterall; I just started off with a *Big Bang*, and the rest has been artful "hands-off" style management called *evolution*. In other words, any solution to living was acceptable, so long as it gave a creature an edge on survival. Evolution did all the work, and I just sat back and kept saying, "OK, so long as it works."

OK, SO LONG AS IT WORKS

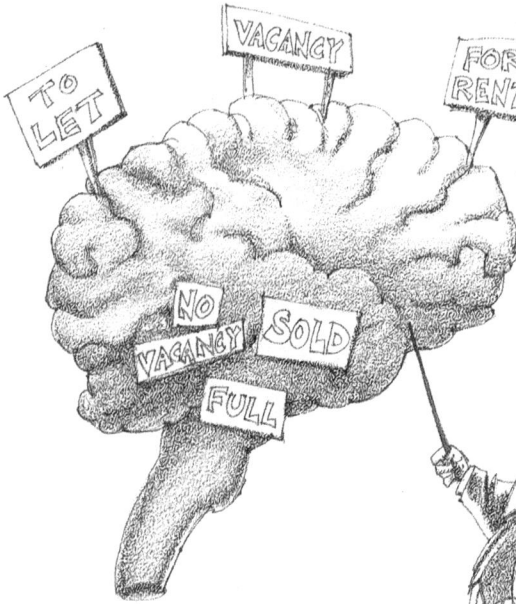

One of the marvels to come out of that evolutionary process was the *human mind*--a wonderfully flexible lump of gubbins that ensured the survival of humans against formidable odds.

The flexibility of the human mind allowed bits to adapt to various local conditions better than any other species.

But this *same flexibility* led humans to create their *own* world which their minds simply *can't cope* with. And now humans are in the process of destroying themselves and the planet they depend on.

Jesus...

Well, even *Jesus* hasn't been able to change your ways all that much--nor have the other big religious, philosophical and scientific figures who have tried to persuade humans to evolve their own consciousnesses.

Your man-made world continues to change *too fast* for your minds to *cope* with. Me and my evolution just *can't keep up!*

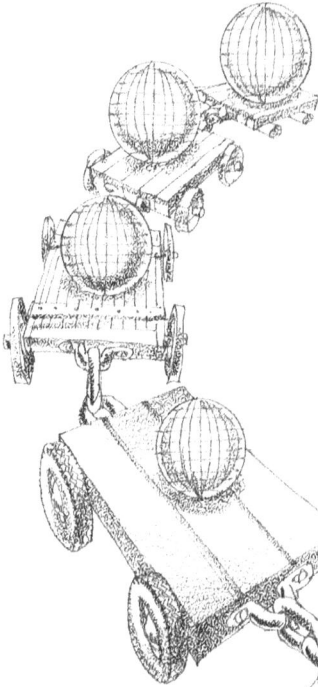

You have a terribly inaccurate picture of what's *really* going on around you, and yet you've got the *whole world* in your hands.

You've treated the world as your toy. The man-made world has *grown* alarmingly, while your mind deals with it as if nothing has changed in millions of years. Evolution can't keep up with your impact on the natural world.

Globe stays the same size while man-made world grows.

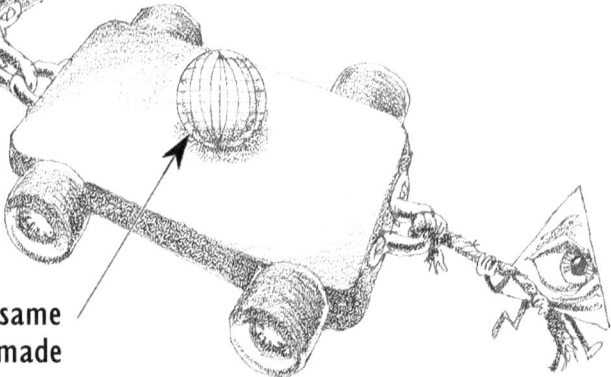

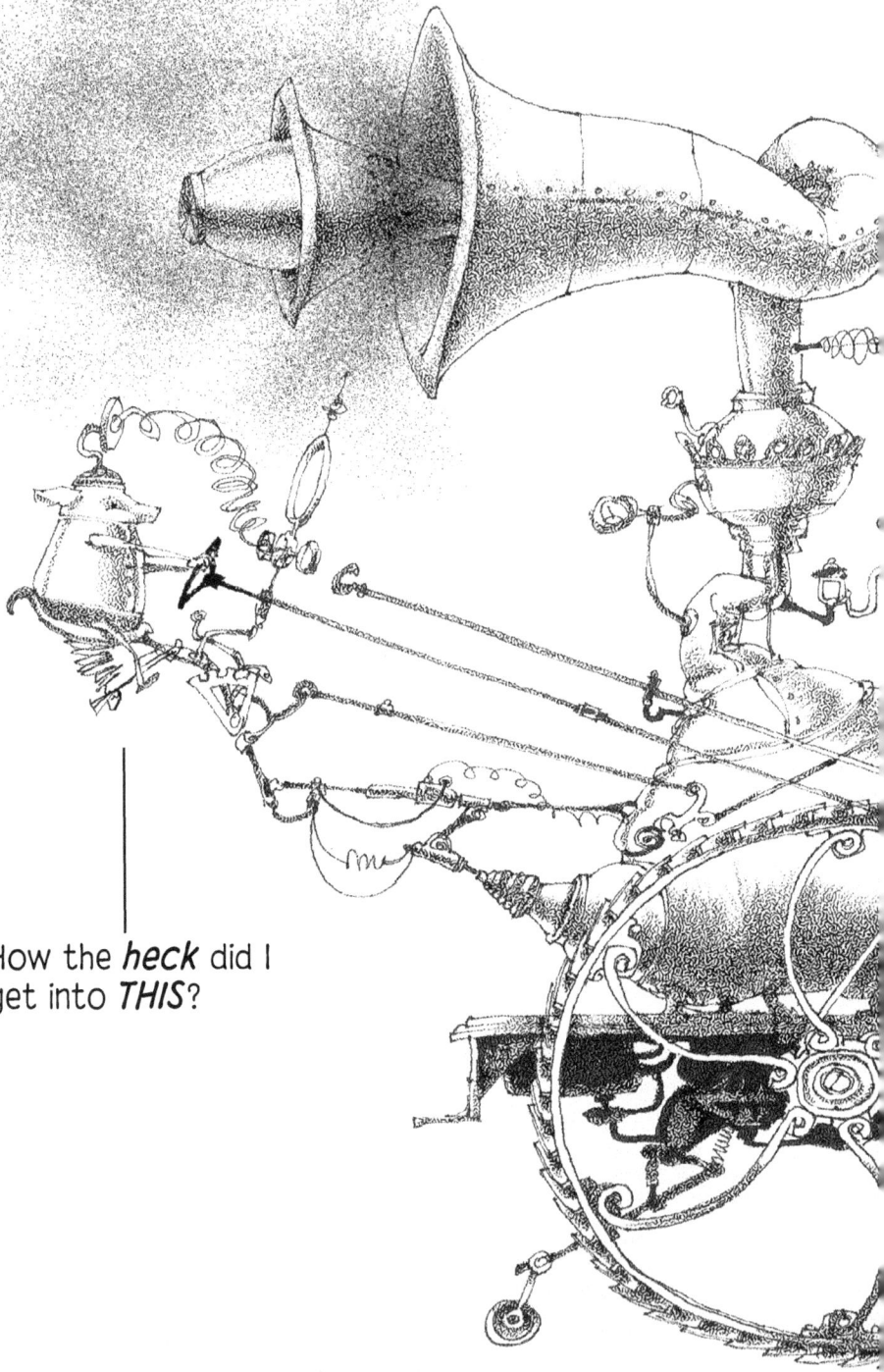

How the *heck* did I
get into *THIS*?

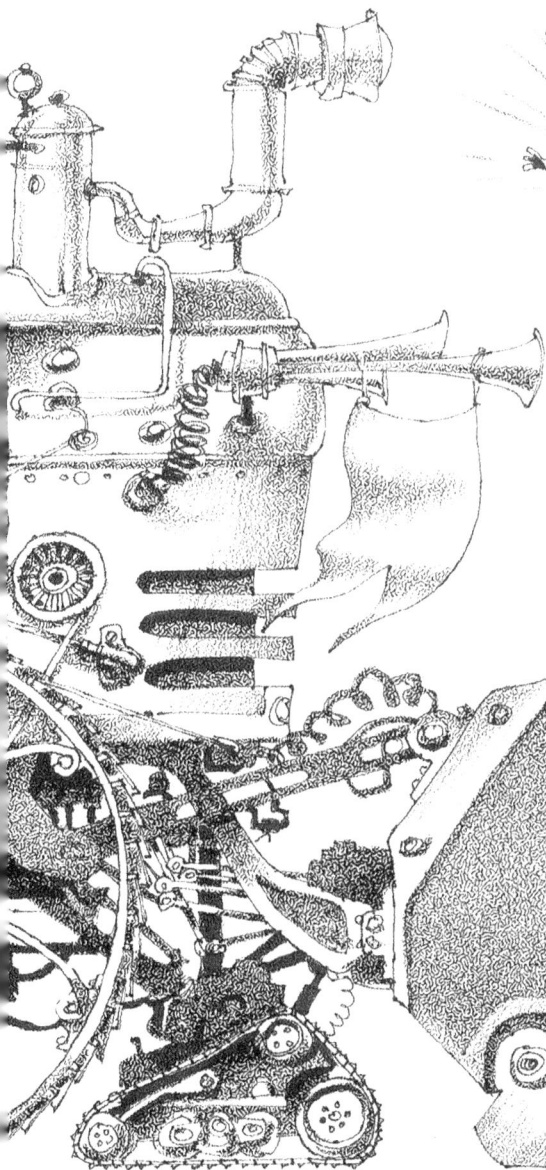

The trouble started
when the *extreme
adaptability* of the
mind set humankind onto
the path of *civilization*.

Now, humans
have created
a world that
*totally
overwhelms*
their minds.

So what can
I possibly do
to **change**
the way things
work around
here?

Well, you'll find it's
almost *impossible*
to control staffing
decisions at Mind
LTD...it's going to take
some *pretty crafty*
management.

A pig-head's ***gotta do*** what
a pig-head's ***gotta do.***

A pig-head's ***gotta do*** what
a pig-head's ***gotta do.***

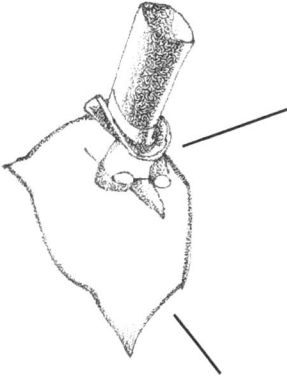

You're dealing with a *very big* company that's been around for *millions of years.* It's hopeless to try to *change* the way those pig-heads work, and you can *forget* about *messing* with company policy.

The only thing you might be able to do is influence who gets *wheeled in* to do *what* job.

Don't be *too upset* with yourself if at first you find it very difficult to change the way things work at Mind LTD.

Just remember, you're fighting *millions of years* of *company policy.*

Good luck--you're gonna *need* it, and you haven't got a whole lot of time to change things before you snuff yourselves out. Now, I'm *outta* here.

What? Y-you're just going to leave me to it? Just when I need you more than ever? Are you *out of your mind*?

I'm not, but *you* most *definitely* are, my friend. . .

...and
so are
you.

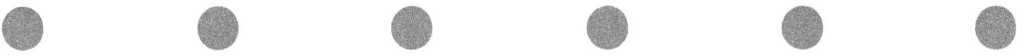

When the first atomic bomb exploded,
Albert Einstein wrote, "Everything has now
changed except for our way of thinking."

6

• • • • • •

A Change of Pace for A Change of Mind

We're out of date.

Think of it this way: The mind is as it is because the world was as it was.

The virtual program needs an update.

Here's my disclaimer for not giving you a surefire program to become a better person in a week. I don't think 10 steps to a better mind is what anybody needs these days, since there are so many rituals out there that can promise everything that you might possibly want to be done. It's what we want to do that's in question. I'll present here another way of looking at what's going on in our lives, and see if the idea that our world of experience is one that we created can help us see a way around our normal habits.

The problem we all have now is like having out-of-date software or keeping a tube-type radio going in the days of the Internet. To look back: 25,000 years ago, the human population was, at most, a few million, surviving mainly by hunting and gathering. The invention of agriculture 10,000 years ago revolutionized the human experience. Settlements grew up along the fertile flood plains of the Nile, in the Fertile Crescent of the Middle East, and around the Ganges Delta and Huang Ho (Yellow River) in Asia. Then they spread throughout the world.

The rise of the human population has been truly extraordinary. At the time of the agricultural revolution, the total human population was less than 10 million; today, that many are born every month. It took from the beginnings of humanity, say a million years ago, to produce the first billion people; and it took far less than two decades to produce the most recent billion! This is important, because the mind evolved to produce a virtual reality of the world of tens of thousands of years ago. But things have changed since then.

When those ancestors began to settle down and till the soil, they started on the road to cities, to overpopulation, to smog and to nuclear weapons. The trip down that road was slow at first; in the 10,000 years from the agricultural revolution to the Middle Ages, there was no great change in the nature of human lives.

In the Industrial Revolution, from the late 18th to the mid-19th centuries, the number of inventions greatly increased: printing presses, factories, steam engines, mass production, railroads, electric power, telegraphs, and more. In this new era, development piled on development, and the pace of change picked up.

Human society moved faster and faster, until it took off into a new and unknown world. Where there were once only prairies and deserts, now farms and factories thrive. Where there were swamps and forests, now high-tech laboratories and launching pads are built. Dreary work that would have taken weeks (say, summing up endless pages of sales and debit accounts) now

EARLY HUMAN

...same as it was for great-great-great grandfather

MILLENNIA

MODERN HUMAN

Woah! Can't deal with this!

ONE DAY

LEVEL OF CHANGE IN ENVIRONMENT

RATE OF CHANGE

Our mind has to deal with a world that presents more shifts and changes in a single day than our ancestors had to deal with over thousands of years.

take a second or two. Work that was impossible in any previous timeframe (say, summing up weather data so it could do society some use) can now be done in minutes.

These changes came late in the day; for most of human history, people were delivered by their parents into a world bounded by a few miles and containing a few hundred individuals. Even now, most people's acquaintances are in the 100-200 range. It was a simple world, and children were taught about it and lived inside that same environment for their entire lives.

MENTAL OBSOLESCENCE
Our mind has remained pretty much the same for millions of years, while the world we have created puts far greater demands on it than in previous eras.

Now the world of our parents isn't our world; the world of our youth, even, isn't the world we grow old within. Anyone who was born in the 1940s or before was born into a world in which a majority of the present countries did not even exist, and less than half the number of people lived on Earth than are alive today. At the time of the birth of our parents or grandparents (those who were over 85 in 2000), there had never been a world war, electricity and pasteurization were rare, and one out of every three people died in childhood.

While all of us were born in the 20th or 21st century, it's important to note what happened just before our time. The world has changed more in the last 10,000 years than in the preceding 4 million years; more in the past century than in the previous 100. On our calendar of human life, science, civilizations, religions, technology and architecture all appear in the last few minutes before midnight of December 31. Our ancestors had thousands, sometimes millions, of years to adapt to smaller changes in the environment than those we now face daily. Modern human development is mental, not physical, evolution; 25,000 years is too fleeting a time for there to be physical adaptation to the radical changes in the environment. In the next two years, more people will be added to the earth's population than lived at the time of Christ.

Our mental system may have been optimal in coping with a stable environment, but in the complex world of today, new situations and changes in their lives often upset people. The conflict between our evolutionary capabilities and the demands placed on us today leads to stress-related ailments such as ulcers. We are forced always to adapt to our own creations -- the airplane, television, nuclear power.

We have not evolved quickly enough to comprehend and solve the problems of the colossal number of people (6.5 billion) that are alive today. We face problems of a scale and speed for which history and biology have left us poorly prepared. Much of what is newly invented or created is now done by a lone genius or a small group, isolated from the rest of us. Therefore, our technology can leap way ahead of the ability of the remaining billions of us to adapt.

The basic faculties of mind, hardware and software -- senses, perception, memory, thought and social judgment -- evolved in a stable, small, simple and slow world, now long gone. We can't sense radiation, or low levels of acid rain, or electromagnetic fields. Today's problems now pose unprecedented, even incalculable dangers.

CAN'T CATCH UP

The world has changed at a pace that our old-world minds cannot hope to catch up with and adapt to properly.

Individuals were more afraid of the first few small atomic bombs than they are of the tens of thousands of much more powerful nuclear weapons that are now in the arsenals of the U.S. and other countries. When First Lady Betty Ford was reported to have breast cancer, women all across the country went to their physicians to get examined. Both reactions are misapplications to immediate and local phenomena. This mental emphasis on new and exciting changes in the world makes individuals, and society as a whole, vulnerable to anyone who can exploit this component of the mind. It leads to the effectiveness of terrorism, to violence spreading as a result of watching brutality on television and in movies, and to ignoring the dangers resulting from acid rain.

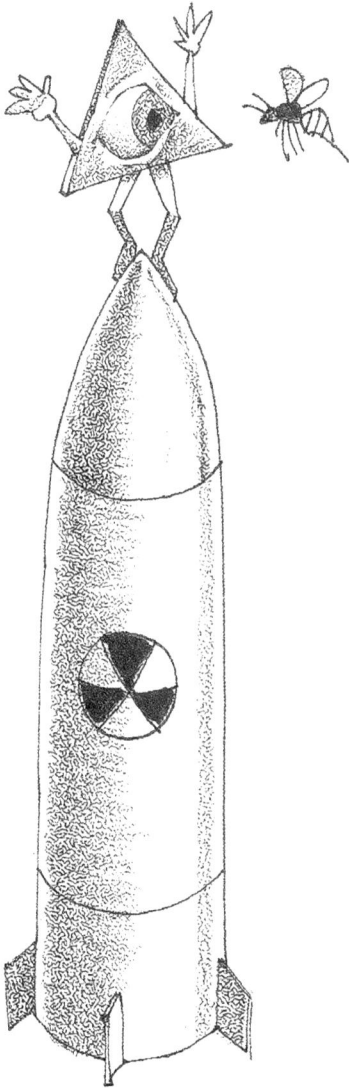

OUR DAILY THREAT

Our minds only notice new threats and ignore constant threats, even when the constant threats are far greater.

We constantly judge things by comparison, and our judgment shifts constantly. An automobile ad may say "Jaguar car prices range from $99,000 to as low as $29,950." This ad cleverly makes your comparison shift, and you begin telling yourself that the $29,950 model is actually quite cheap for a Jag. Before the ad, you might have been thinking of spending $16,000 for a VW. When you decide on the $29,995 Jag, you suddenly find it's surprisingly inexpensive to get a flat-screen TV for only $1,400. MindReal shifts, as in this case, when more expensive items are put into the hopper. So on vacation we're less likely to worry about the cost of dinner, since we've spent so much on traveling expenses. And this same old routine, designed to simplify our experience of the world, comes into play with the billions spent in government (after all, what's one more measly billion in a trillion-dollar economy?).

We're insensitive to continuing problems, since they don't change enough to trigger a virtual response to them. It's like not seeing the nose in front of us. (It's still there.) I was once observing people in a rest home, and found that about a third had emphysema brought on by the pollution from a Midwest refinery. The pollution is so slow and constant that few notice it, but it costs the country millions of lives and countless dollars, not to mention pain and suffering. This is a far greater, on-going, and more important tragedy than a single terrorist murder; yet it's scarcely as attention-grabbing as sensational murder trials or the antics of rock stars.

Crack cocaine is a huge societal problem, and the airwaves and newspapers are surfeited with information on how dangerous it is. We know crack is addictive and a killer. Another drug, which is six times as addictive as crack and will kill 3-5 million people in this decade, should make you concerned. But this drug is in a cigarette, and since it is a continuing killer and part of our environment, it gets little attention. Not much is done about the chronic dangers of highway safety or the 300 murders per week or the 100 billion cigarettes smoked each year -- because they are familiar problems.

The mind wheels; it is not stable. But we have a difficult time seeing this in ourselves. It wheels from condition to condition, from emergency to happiness, from quiescence to concern. As it wheels to different states, it selects the various components of mind which operate in those states. All stretched, the mind wheels to include its moving selection process; it wheels into play segments that are designed for quite limited and specific

WHEEL AWARE

Knowing the mind wheels is the first step to successful self-observation.

purposes, such as a comparison program for judging weight or an innate emotional routine for acting upon anger.

Some points on self-observing may be relevant here. As these examples indicate, it's important to notice the tremendous effect of mood on your current situation. The old metaphor of rose-colored glasses is really true. That's why we make such misjudgments when, for instance, we fall in love with a person, a new house, a new country. "How could I have thought...?" we all say later.

There's no complete solution save becoming a bloodless robot, but we can perhaps write down some of our thoughts when either elated or deflated, and see how we judge the same events (our finances, the attractiveness of our mate, our job accomplishments) so differently without any "real" reason. Knowing that the mind wheels is the first step; seeing some of those wheels in retrospect is the second. Third, and perhaps almost impossible, would be knowing what's wheeling in, and why, when it happens. Some people say they can get to this; but, like running a marathon, one needs to begin.

Knowledge of our decision-making and attention processes makes some of the ways we respond to events more comprehensible. Simply put, because the virtual reality we live in notes only sharp changes in the world, human beings are not easily able to register threatening changes that are not immediate emergencies. The typical response is to attend closely to the first occurrence of an event, then tune out as we habituate. This happens in responding to a noise, to a sudden appearance of the sun from behind a cloud, and to extreme danger.

The same mental routines that evolved in a simple, stable world are far too often overwhelmed in today's complex world. Virtual reality programs that evolved to judge brightness are used today to judge prices. But what to do now?

If minds have been changed by the world they live in, as are the minds of a Peruvian weaver and a Japanese sumo, then certainly we can change ours by calling on unused capacities in our culture. Most change will come from new information and new media. In the past, we've simply read about a world, giving those with abstract skills a high status in schools and in the workplace. Today most students can get access to understandable information at any time. Along with the resultant decline in reading, though, can come a new appreciation of the relationships between individuals, countries and us. Education will be the key.

UNSTABLE MIND

Our mind has no idea just how unstable it is--it labors under the illusion that it is thinking in a "straight line," when the truth is that it is far more unstable.

We also need a new curriculum about human nature, one that looks at different cultures' abilities and tries to communicate them throughout the world. The more we understand how the mind lives and what capacities lie dormant, developed or over-developed in each of us, the quicker we can remake ourselves. Again, in this modern world, communications will play a great role, giving us access to libraries and instructional materials on-line.

A global "patriotism" is already replacing local boosters. Germany and Italy, for instance, in their modern forms, are only a few hundred years old, and Europe as a political entity is looming. Instead of focusing on local "baby down the sewer" stories, we need to storm the media to create demands for information on long-term, large-scale events, such as global pollution and climate change, as well as population and technology trends that affect us all.

We need to change not only the content of the media to a large extent, but also to change the media themselves, allowing more interactive learning with the use of computers in schools and at home, in childhood and in adulthood.

We need to teach people not only to get information into their minds, but also to change the way they think. One might call two major kinds of information-gathering "text and context." Ever since the ancient Greeks, we've increasingly elaborated the "text" approach to life, literally and figuratively -- reducing experience to words and reducing those words to the literal value of information. But this ignores the surroundings and implications of our actions, the way events influence each other, the way we influence and interact with each other.

Again, we don't fully understand, for instance, that other cultures have different values than we do. They see events more in relation to each other, rather than the isolated analysis that we teach. More limiting, too, is to assume that "scientific logical thinking" or "lawyerly thinking" is the only way to deal with the world.

Consider a recent psychological study by Richard Nesbitt and colleagues. He and a collaborator presented Chinese and U.S. students with everyday contradictions. For instance, a daughter plans to leave home early. The Americans tended to take sides ("mothers should respect daughters' independence"); whereas the Chinese felt a middle way was appropriate -- that mothers and daughters have failed to understand each other.

And if the mind is constantly "primed" by our everyday experiences, we need to expand the basis of information available to us, to create, like the Chinese above, other possibilities.

The mind is a set of possibilities awaiting awakening by the world, and it should be our job to find these and to communicate them. One form of this communication is specially designed literature and the sayings of some of the spiritual and philosophical greats. The problem is that books such as the Bible and the Torah are too exposed, and we stop listening. Thus, reading about Jesus in the noncanonical Gospel of Thomas offers a striking awakening of another great teaching. The exceptional literature collected by Idries Shah from 1964–1996 are "teaching-stories" that are designed to take the mind along unfamiliar routes, perhaps to "prime" it to rendezvous with reality in a different manner.

These are stories read and reread by countless generations. There are even children's stories based on them. They have been developed by people, perhaps somewhat wiser than the rest of us, to prepare their minds for the unforeseen and to extend their conception of what they can do. In other words, they take the unconscious and random priming that goes on everyday -- the conversations, the advertising, the general level of discourse -- and offer an alternative to, and even a "way out" of, confined thinking. I have continually recommended Shah's books, and they are on recommended reading lists. They should be part of the new curriculum on human nature which we need to develop. They often provide a "shock" that restructures our private reality.

I will close with one example from Shah's *Caravan of Dreams*.

Seeing Double

A FATHER said to his double-seeing son:

"Son, you see two instead of one."

"How can that be?" the boy replied. "If I were, there would seem to be four moons up there in place of two."

Idries Shah
Caravan of Dreams

Some Recent Suggested Readings

Richard E. Cytowic
The Man Who Tasted Shapes
Bradford, New York, 1998

Merlin Donald
A Mind so Rare: the Evolution of Human Consciousness
Norton, New York, 2001

Dan Schacter
The Seven Sins of Memory
Houghton Mifflin, Boston, 2001

Older References

Robert Allison
Minds in Many Pieces
Rawson-Wade, New York, 1980

Robert Ornstein
The Evolution of Consciousness
Prentice-Hall, New York, 1994

Idries Shah
"Seeing Double"
from *Caravan of Dreams*
Octagon Press, London, original edition 1968

Ben Libet
"Neuronal vs. Subjective Timing for a Conscious Experience"
in *Cerebral Correlates of Conscious Experience*
Buser & Rouseul-Buser (Eds.)
Elsevier, Amsterdam, 1975

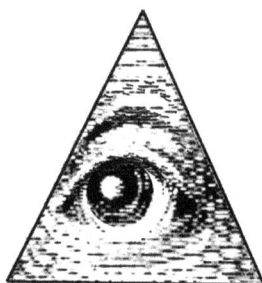

www.ingramcontent.com/pod-product-compliance
Lightning Source LLC
Chambersburg PA
CBHW080419030426
42335CB00020B/2502